SURFING THE
SEA OF CHI

SURFING THE SEA OF CHI

To Mary,
May you always walk
in balance.
Lea Williamson

LEA WILLIAMSON

Indigo River Publishing

Indigo River Publishing
3 West Garden Street, Ste. 352
Pensacola, FL 32502
www.indigoriverpublishing.com

Editors: Samantha Nelson and Regina Cornell
Cover & Book Design: mycustombookcover.com

Ordering Information:
Quantity sales: Special discounts are available on quantity purchases by corporations, associations, and others. For details, contact the publisher at the address above.

Orders by US trade bookstores and wholesalers: Please contact the publisher at the address above.

Printed in the United States of America

Library of Congress Control Number: 2019947047

ISBN: 978-1-950906-13-0

First Edition

With Indigo River Publishing, you can always expect great books, strong voices, and meaningful messages. Most importantly, you'll always find . . . words worth reading.

Contents

Are you breathing? Are you aware that you are breathing? If you feel, as many today do, that it is difficult to simply catch your breath in our tumultuous, fear-filled world, you have come to the right place for inspiration. The words on the following pages emerged hoping to find you, to bring you a full breath of fresh air. May they inspire you to let go, to breathe, to relax, and to be the solution.

It wasn't until I started writing Surfing the Sea of Chi and I read the words on the page that I realized how profound the last ten years of learning to surf had been for me. Surfing, tai chi, and the Tao completely transformed me and restored my soul, reconnecting me to the source and the magical mystery of it all.

I am so grateful for the sheer transformative power surfing can have on the individual and the planet that I am giving 1 percent of my profits from this book back to the grassroots environmental work of the Surfrider Foundation's Sebastian Inlet chapter. As a surfer, I am grateful to have access to waves, just one of the many ocean-minded projects embraced by the nonprofit Surfrider Foundation. If you surf, live by the beach, or just want to be part of the ocean solution, I encourage you to become a part of this volunteer-led organization and help keep our beaches clean, protected, and accessible to all. Even if you live in the heartland, your local waterways eventually flow to the ocean, so the health of your waters also makes a difference.

Thank you for being part of the solution and for being part of the unified field we all share. I'm grateful for you.

The Tao that can be told is not the eternal Tao.
The name that can be named is not the eternal name.
The nameless is the beginning of heaven and earth.
The named is the mother of the thousand things.
Ever desireless one can see the mystery.
Ever desiring one can see the manifestations.
—Lao Tzu, Tao Te Ching

To surf is to connect to the source energy, the Nameless, the beginning of heaven and earth. To ride a wave well is to have the
energy of the cosmos move you through time and space with effortless
grace. To surf is to connect with the Tao. To become a surfer is, for the
mindful, to become a Taoist at heart, and even in ritual.

These were things I didn't understand when I decided to take
up surfing. Rather, I made a very practical decision to get over my
lifelong, irrational fear of water by distracting myself with the very
physical activity of surfing. This somehow made sense in my mind.
Sometimes it does make sense to face one's fear.

When I first walked out into the warm, shallow, calm waters of Cocoa Beach, Florida, as a forty-year-old grom (short for *grommet*, or novice surfer), the fear gripped my heart like a boxer's closing fist. It was ridiculous, really. Even in clear, waist-deep water, surrounded by splashing tourists, with lifeguards on shore, and even though I had a full-body flotation device in my hands in the form of a borrowed surfboard and my best friend (an extreme water woman) at my side, I was utterly, breathlessly terrified. The fear was too much for me to bear. In fact, the fear and the anticipation of the fear had taken my breath away and I struggled to catch it. I didn't realize this one choice to leave my comfort zone and meet my fear head-on would shape my life and teach me the lessons of the Tao.

To fully describe surfing is impossible. To simply say what surfing is can't be done. This is how I know that surfing is a pathway to Tao. Ask any surfer and they will tell you it's impossible to put the experience of a great ride into words. "Only a surfer knows" is an easily understood and agreed-upon sentiment by those who dare to paddle out. So it is to know the Tao: impossible to describe, impossible to fully understand as well. We can catch glimpses of its true nature, have moments of clarity, but when it comes right down to it, our limited human minds simply cannot comprehend the big picture of what it means to live the surf lifestyle nor of what the Tao is.

At the time I just wanted to get over it, this crippling, utterly ridiculous fear. I had never had an unpleasant experience in the water or been present when someone else did. Yet this primal, paralyzing fear closed around me whenever I entered water. Even the shallow end of a swimming pool gave me pause, for goodness' sake, and that's just absurd. Living in Florida, a state surrounded by water, this fear really wasn't healthy for my physical survival, not to mention my social survival. I remember evading gatherings that were water focused as a teenager. The numerous pool parties, beach luaus, and boating trips that permeate social life in coastal Florida were all outside of my comfort zone and therefore beyond my grasp.

This fear had limited me my whole life, and I was sick and tired of it. I decided to confront it head-on—I was going to learn how to surf. This, I reasoned, would give me a physical and mental distraction from the fear that I was in continual jeopardy while traversing that terrifying, watery realm. So, at forty years old, on a sunny summer morning, surfboard tethered to my ankle, I slowly walked into the shallows of the Atlantic Ocean on Cocoa Beach.

My fearless friend Mersea (which she pronounced "mercy" or "merci" with a slight French accent) coached me as we waded out together. Instead of trying to paddle out to where the other surfers were in the lineup (where you sit waiting and watching for waves), we slowly walked out to stand in stomach-deep water and catch a few broken waves. She advised riding them lying on my stomach, not trying to stand up. This was excellent advice. Go slow, don't rush—just like tai chi training had taught me. Just this hint of familiarity gave me comfort in the ever-shifting water that had been my nemesis since childhood.

Mersea understood that if I didn't enjoy my first session, it would be difficult for me to continue trying to surf. She made sure the conditions were mild and not even slightly intimidating the first day we went out. Looking back, I would now call the conditions that day one foot, glassy, and weak with hardly enough ripple for seasoned surfers to get in the water. But Mersea understood the intensity and depth of my fear. She also understood my purpose in learning to surf and was wise enough to start me off slow.

She set me up to just enjoy the sensation of the energy pushing the wave, with no expectations of paddling out or standing up on the board. What a good teacher. Sometimes I see boyfriends trying to teach their girlfriends without understanding this simple concept: it should be super easy and enjoyable, especially the first few times. The surf conditions matter a lot for this, which is why I sometimes refer to myself as a fair-weather surfer. I only go when the conditions are right for me, not necessarily when everyone else is out charging it.

I'll never forget that first day riding tiny waves like a kid on a boogie board. It left me giddy with bubbling excitement and most definitely wanting more. Once I was comfortable simply being in waist- to stomach-deep water (which took about fifteen minutes to let go of my panicked breathing), then Mersea left my side, catching a small wave, and glided in on her belly toward the shore in a demonstration of how to start. The very thought of her having left me standing there in about four feet of water was unsettling. I had no human safety line beside me. I calmed my breath again and pushed off the sandy ocean bottom to catch a little white water from a small, already-broken wave. The wave left me behind and kept rolling to shore. I did not catch my first wave. Timing certainly plays a factor in this, I thought. At the time I didn't realize how much I had to learn to surf.

We spent a couple of joy-filled hours bellyboarding in on some tiny midsummer Florida wavelets. How patient a friend to forgo surfing herself so I would feel comfortable and have a buddy nearby for my first purposeful, fear-filled encounter with the ocean. When I was ready for a break and went in to shore, Mersea paddled over to the lineup and promptly caught a few stand-up waves as if it were a cakewalk. Her beautiful, skilled, effortless style made many heads turn as she easily glided around all others in the tourist-filled shallows. Mersea had been surfing since she was seven years old. She'd traveled all over the world in pursuit of her chosen sport: Fiji, Japan, Mexico, Indonesia, and Hawaii, of course. Being in the water with her as my guide was a comfort and blessing to overcoming my irrational fear.

Sitting on the hard, compacted beach sand and sipping water while watching Mersea play in her domain, I wanted even more to learn to surf. Now that I'd had a small taste of riding waves and the sheer joy of it and I was seeing how beautiful a skilled woman riding a longboard was, I was totally hooked. I knew I could one day surf like that and be just as "in the flow." But it would take some time and be a slow progression—yet another parallel with my tai chi training.

If only for this reason, I know surfing is Taoist: it can easily reconnect us to the fresh, childlike joy of life and the cyclical nature of it.

Years of practicing tai chi had taught me how to laugh at my mistakes; to let go of my controlling, pride-filled adult ego; to become unburdened as a child—this is one reason we're most commonly called tai chi players over other monikers. We don't work out, we play tai chi. In most of my classes we typically laugh and have fun while we practice our slow tai chi flow.

This first taste of surfing had also brought me childlike joy and a sense of freedom I certainly hadn't expected to find in that big, terrifying ocean. There was a simple, pure pleasure in letting the wave (energy of the earth and stars) push me through space. I saw it as a free, natural energy ride, like coasting downhill on a bike, skiing or snowboarding down the side of a mountain, or sailing. It takes us away from the effort and struggles of life in the contrived, man-made world. This was, in a sense, the same driving force that pushed Nikola Tesla forward to explore the possibilities of harnessing the free, natural energy that is always around us. If you've ever glided down a hill on a bike or some such free-energy ride, I'm sure you'll agree that there really is nothing more emancipating to our clock- and boundary-controlled lives than being moved *through* nature *by* nature.

To do this is to go with the flow. To go with the flow and use the energy of that flow with grace and style takes quite a bit more effort than one day at the beach (or one year of tai chi). Like all beginners, young or otherwise, this has not come easily for me. I push, I fight, I resist. I use too much force and muscle. I try too hard to exert control instead of just letting go. Yet with patience and persistence, the flow and grace will come. This is the promise of Tao: keep consciously engaging in your practice and the energy of that practice will eventually work its way in you until one day you are no longer practicing tai chi; it is flowing through you, like a wave of energy that moves through water.

When you watch surfers paddle out, it's easy to tell who we groms are. We muscle our way through the breaking waves, looking less than graceful. Our legs are not pulled together, streamlining aerodynamically with the surfboard, but spread-eagled like a starfish, creating more resistance; our arms splash about with too much effort, trying to force our way through the water. We groms often don't get very far very fast. We are easily out-paddled by more experienced surfers, and we wear out quickly, often having to go back to shore without ever making it beyond the breaking whitewash. Because we use too much force, the resistance of incoming waves beats us down. With determined practice we learn that when we relax, when we don't force it, when we think it through, study the incoming wave, feel the undercurrent, and understand the direction of the flow, then when the resistance comes (and it will eventually come) we can position ourselves for the least impact, relax, and just let the storm of whitewash pass by before we resume our efforts to paddle forward. This, in Taoism and tai chi practice, is called *yield and overcome*. With diligent practice, surfing will lead us to the Tao.

There's a classic scene in the original *Point Break* movie where a cute, blond preteen surfer boy working at a surf shop says this very thing to an FBI detective who wants to learn to surf so he can catch a criminal: "Surfing is the source. It will change your life forever." I had no idea how true these words were when I first heard them. Now I know because, like the FBI detective, learning to surf forever altered my life. I didn't know when I started that it would happen this way. I just wanted to get past my intense fear of water, not become a Taoist soul-surfer riding galactic waves of chi.

Yield and overcome.
Bend and be straight.
Empty and be full.
Wear out and be new.
Have little and gain.
Have much and be confused.
—Lao Tzu, Tao Te Ching

The first summer I spent learning to surf, I took every opportunity to be out in the ocean. Many times, I went in the water without a surfboard, just trying to face my fear and control my panic-filled breathing. Luckily for me, the slope of the bottom surface at Cocoa Beach is super gradual. One can walk out beyond the fishing pier with her head still above water when the tide is low. This gave me a great deal of comfort, knowing it wasn't that deep out there. While Mersea preferred to surf in deeper water, I embraced the safety net of being able to put my feet down and simply stand up any time I wanted to. I felt like it would be impossible for me to drown that way; how naive about the ocean I was.

But I so wanted to get in! How beautiful it was on that calm, sunny day—like bathing in crystalline blue-green light. When sunlight passes through clean, clear water reflecting a sandy bottom, it's difficult to resist plunging in. But resist I always had, until now. I wanted so very badly to casually ease into that inviting, warm water. Instead, what I got whenever I walked into it were shivers of fear lightly quaking my core muscles, followed promptly by very shallow gasping that persisted for minutes after exiting my liquid tormentor. Frequently I would simply freeze in my sinking sandy tracks, my arms drawn in hugging myself in a protective embrace, before I could slowly shuffle deeper again.

It was utterly ridiculous. All around me in the clear, shallow waters of popular, gentle Cocoa Beach were frolicking children, round people bobbing up and down, floating like fishing bobbers, and pasty-white tourists of all ages boogie boarding. How could it be that I alone was so thoroughly terrified in this water? It defied all reason and rationality. But there it was, every single time I got in up to my waist—for a few months, anyway: the fear controlled me much more than I could contain it. It held me so tightly in its frightful grasp that it felt like fear alone would crush me from the inside, bones and all. The intensity of it just wasn't healthy, and I was determined to overcome it as one would slowly study, stalk, and subdue a beast. It would take time and courage. I knew that the longer I had let this monster grow, the stronger it had become over me. It made sense that it would take time to conquer it as well. Thankfully, tai chi had taught me patience, persistence, and perseverance.

It didn't take long for me to discover just how complex an act wave riding really is. While constantly battling my heart-gripping fear, I was also learning how to read the waves, offer the least possible resistance, stay balanced on the surfboard when paddling out, how to sit on the board and not fall over when waiting for waves, and how to catch a wave. As planned, my mind was now a bit distracted from the fear because of all the elements of surfing I had to think about, but fear still had the leading role in my surfing experience.

One of the biggest helps to controlling this fear was regulating my breathing. I realized that every time I got in any body of water, my breathing became shallow to the point of nonexistence, constrained, and very rapid. My tai chi and qigong teachers had taught me that the breath can control the emotions. I put that ancient knowledge to work for me. I usually walked or rode my bike a mile and a half down the beach to work; so throughout that warm summer, when there was no surf, after work I'd just walk out chest deep into the ocean and work on my panicked breathing.

The simplest, most powerful breathing practice I ever learned, I got from my first exposure to tai chi: stand, relax, breathe. It was one of the first lessons in a VHS video of tai chi Yang short form. Stand in the ready stance: feet shoulder-width apart, knees bent softly, elongated spine, and arms out and round at the sides like an old West sheriff ready to draw. "Stand, relax, breathe" still is the most profound practice I do, even after twenty years of fancy footwork and tai chi training. The simplest of all is the most profound. Less is more. Now I used this technique under duress in the ever-shifting currents of the central Florida Atlantic shoreline. Stand. Relax. Breathe. Slow down, be still. Relax, let go. Breathe fully, in and out.

Gradually, this practice worked to regulate my shallow, fast panic breath. Over time, I was able to turn that spastic, out-of-control fear breathing into slow, full, continuous, flowing breaths. This simple technique did in fact calm my fear while standing vulnerably all alone in the ocean. The mindfulness of this standing meditation allowed me to focus on the inner space of my mindbody (breathing, posture, muscle tension) instead of focusing on the outer space of the treacherous water I was in.

This is the mindfulness of simply being instead of doing. This standing meditative practice is a type of qigong (*qi*, or *chi* = breath, *gong* = work). I had learned it but hadn't practiced much of it outside of class. Instead, I focused more on the active, moving tai chi instead of the still, meditative practices of qigong. The two typically go together in tai chi training to create more balance and harmony using both action and inaction. When I first started, I was more interested in the active tai chi practices. Now, the inactive practice of "stand, relax, breathe" was helping me engage in the highly active practice of surfing. The balance of the Tao, the yin and yang of it all, makes me smile. I was to learn more about this soon.

You've experienced fear or panic accompanied by a change in breathing. Many people have had an incident or two of this in their lives, and a few unfortunate souls have regular panic attacks. Some people hyperventilate in panic. Their rate of respiration accelerates but becomes shallow and nonrhythmic. Others, like me, hypoventilate with fear. Our rate of respiration drops when we panic, or we simply stop breathing altogether, and we may struggle to catch our breath. The fear takes our breath away. So, this is where my surfer's journey really began after the thrill of bellyboarding had already drawn me in. I absolutely had to control my fear breathing, and I did it with "stand, relax, breathe."

If I couldn't breathe for fear in the water, there's certainly no way I could engage in the extremely physical act of surfing. An almost unconscious plan of action was born: get control of my breathing first. Within a month or two I was able to breathe normally while standing in waist-deep water. Now I was doing ridiculous-looking things like simply standing in water as deep as I could touch, with my friend's surfboard, rather than trying to paddle, float, or surf. While I let myself be terrified, I breathed in and out as slowly and deeply as I could.

That's it. Just standing out there for twenty or thirty minutes in deep, flat, wakeless water breathing slow, deep breaths with the safety net of a surfboard floating near my head. Stand. Relax. Breathe.

Did I look ridiculous? Absolutely. Was it scary? You betcha. I found it utterly terrifying. Did I get hurt? Not in the least. Not only was I breathing my fear away, my rational mind was also learning with each water experience that nothing was going to hurt me. I was not going to be mysteriously sucked under the water by a swirling vortex or sawed in half by the jaws of some mammoth unseen oceanic beast. But if my breath hadn't calmed me, my rational mind would have never recognized that, because my primitive fear took precedence over intellectual reason.

It took several months, but by focusing on slow, deep breathing I was able to lie on the surfboard and paddle out to water so deep my toes couldn't touch the bottom, which was a big and frightening deal for me. To be in water this deep made me panic, and my breathing showed it. After I had paddled past the breaking waves, out into the lineup, I was usually breathing extremely fast, erratically, and from my mouth, like a scared, panting dog. So I'd just sit there on my surfboard a while, calming and deepening my breath, until the fear of being in deep water would subside. Sit. Relax. Breathe. It's fascinating that the basic act of breathing can affect our emotions and overall state of mind so powerfully.

Breathing is the single most important thing we do in life. It's the very first thing we do in this world—to take a breath, to become inspired and cry out that we're here, we made it. And it's the very last thing we do in this life—to breathe out our last breath, to expire. Most people exhale and then die—fascinating. Breathe in to start life; breathe out to end it. The life between these fateful in, out breaths is filled every minute with the physical act of breathing, over and over and over again. We never stop until we're done here. According to the American Lung Association website, on average we humans breathe twenty thousand times a day. Over a seventy-two-year lifespan, that's 483,840,000 breaths in the average American life.

Let's think of breathing from an unfamiliar perspective. How often does the average Joe eat, and how long can Joe live without food? For most of us average Joes, it would be anywhere from four to nine painful, torturous, excruciating months without food before we eventually expired. How long can we go without drinking water? For most, three to five days. How long can we go without breathing? Typically, it's about five minutes. So, our breathing is more important than the food we obsess over with our nonstop shopping, planning, preparing, cooking, storing, couponing, and going out of the way for. Obvious too is that breathing is more important than water, which we also go to extremes for, now more than ever. I know an average Joe who paid $6,000 for a brand-name water system to clean his tap water. That's a lot of money for a blue-collar worker to treat something he already pays for just to have it flow out of the tap. When I asked him if he knew any breathing exercises, he took a couple of big breaths and said, "What's there to know? Even babies know how to breathe."

That's a typical response when I ask people about breathing. They simply have never given it any thought beyond "the lungs are the organs that hold air." Yet there is quite a bit to know about the breath of life, which is what every single breath is. You might think the study of breathing is limited to respiratory therapists and physicians who specialize in the lungs. However, these academics usually know very few breathing exercises beyond taking two or three big breaths, just like my friend the house painter.

My boss at the time, a well-known member of the local "health care" community, we'll call him Dr. D, started making large profits by promoting a food supplement. The protocol he advocated was to take the supplement, which he stood to profit from, and do breathing exercises. This, he claimed, was absolutely proven in clinical testing to show amazing health benefits across the board. At the conclusion of his employee training presentation/sales pitch, I asked, "What breathing exercises?"

Dr. D replied uncertainly, "Uh, I don't know . . . just take some deep breaths, you know." He was not very authoritative nor knowledgeable about the protocol he was promoting. I'm not blaming Dr. D for his lack of knowledge. I totally understand the issue: there's simply no profit in breathing.

Who stands to profit from promoting breathing exercises? Not really anyone except the patient/person doing the breathing. What would compel someone working for profit to learn about nonprofitable breathing? Nothing. Instead, breathing exercise has become a specialized and often misunderstood field. But it's not a new field by any means. People have been experimenting with breathing since the beginning of human history. Traditional breathing experts aren't called doctor or therapist or researcher. They fall under the limited and stereotypical labels of yogi, shaman, kahuna, qigong/tai chi master, monk, or medicine man. Historically, they have not been taken seriously by mainstream medical society, although, I'm happy to say, that is slowly changing. These are the world's leading experts on breathing; always have been and still are. It is due to the breathing techniques I learned from qigong and tai chi that I was able to overcome my lifelong fear, not only of water but also of letting go and learning to flow in life.

You have likely experienced some fear, even irrational fear, in your life: fear of sharks or spiders, fear of small and dark places, fear of being alone or that you're not alone when you should be. Your heart starts to beat hard and fast against your ribs and spine, beating so fast it leaps up, threatening to pound its way right out of your throat. You feel the flood of adrenaline as your body goes on high alert, and your eyes start to bug out of your head to take in all the potential dangers. Your breathing becomes uncontrollable, and you want to be free of your own skin. Hopefully, this has only happened to you on a few occasions. If this is a recurring condition in your life, you can use breath work to overcome those fears. Or, like me, you'd like to get rid of a fear that leaves you breathless.

The wondrous thing about breath work is that every one of us breathes every minute of every day, so with each breath, we have an opportunity to practice. Translation: we can practice anytime, anywhere, in any situation—*any* situation, even a stressful one like learning to surf when scared out your mind. Which is exactly what I did—I focused on slow and very full breaths in and out of the nose, not forced but full, deep breaths. These full, slow, deep, continuous breaths help to calm the central nervous system whether we're in a stressed "fight or flight" mode or a restful "relaxation response" mode. Slow, deep breathing is often associated with meditation and sleeping, so it makes sense that it calms us. The opposite is also true: a fast, erratic breath panics us.

The most stress-free of humans here on the planet, babies, breathe full, deep belly breaths. Meditators breathe slowly with full, deep breaths. Doctors often advise their patients to take slow, deep breaths. Breathing slow and deep has a myriad of health benefits. Unfortunately, some people falsely believe they must use harmful pharmaceuticals to attain the many benefits we get from simply breathing well. A full breath has been linked to better digestion and elimination (no laxative required); conversely, not breathing deeply contributes to constipation. Blood pressure lowers when breathing is calm; the opposite is also true: blood pressure is higher when breathing is fast. It's well known that a slow, full breath can often slow down a fast heart rate, while a fast, shallow breath increases heart strain. I could go on, but it would take quite a while to list all the yin-yang health benefits and side effects of a healthy versus unhealthy breath. Not only is a relaxed, full breath essential for physical health, but it directly affects mental health as well. Taoist master Mantak Chia praises the humble respiratory muscle the diaphragm as lifting the heart and fanning the fires of digestion and metabolism. The diaphragm plays an unrecognized role in our overall health, vitality, and well-being.

Those who do not breathe well typically live in anxiety. Because the respiratory system is connected to most of the body's sensory nerves, any excessive negative stimulus in the environment influences breathing and thus our overall mental and physical health. If you're always exposed to yelling and anger, for example, it can create shortness of breath, resulting over time in deterioration of both physical and mental health. This can happen very slowly over many years and be almost imperceptible. The relationship between health, anxiety, and breathing is a lot more obvious in people who have panic attacks.

Maybe you've seen someone have a panic attack or experienced one yourself. The most obvious outward sign is the breath: it's fast, erratic, shallow, and out of control. Often an observer may offer a paper bag for the person panicking to breathe into. The paper bag focuses the person's mind on his breathing instead of what the panic is about. The paper bag lets the person see his breath as the bag expands and collapses, allowing the primal mind to unconsciously calm the breath to a more normal one; that's when the panic begins to pass, when the breath becomes calmer, fuller, slower. The panic and the erratic breath feed each other. The meditation and the slow, deep breath feed each other as well. The quality of the breath and the quality of the life feed each other. When we deepen the breath, we can deepen the experience of life. I was proving it to myself by being able to experience one of the most enriching activities I've ever had: surfing.

I practice breath work all the time now: sitting in my car at a light, standing in line at the grocery store, waiting for my partner or a co-worker. I especially like breath work right before walking into a situation I expect to be a little stressful, like an interview or a meeting; for some it might be a family get-together. While I now know a lot of different qigong breathing techniques from years of study, all that's not necessary to simply clear and calm the mindbody. Stand (or sit) with good posture. Relax the muscles as much as possible. Breathe mindfully. This works fine. Keep it simple. Less is more.

Simply becoming aware of breathing will change the breath pattern into a healthier one. If you find your emotions escalating and can't escape the situation, just remind yourself that you are breathing. This will typically make the breath fuller, slower, and more even. Breath work doesn't have to be complicated to have a significant impact on how we feel, overall. Breathing is the most important bodily function we have. Our inhale is said to reflect our ability to embrace the moment, to take it all in; our exhale is said to be connected to our ability to let go. Breath masters understand that breathing alone can be used to heal the physical body, open the energetic pathways (meridians), cleanse and restore the energetic centers (chakras, or *dan tiens*), alter current emotions, clear emotional trauma, and balance and enhance brain functions, opening the mind to new perspectives of reality and thus altering consciousness.

In his noteworthy book *Tao of Natural Breathing*, Dennis Lewis expounds that by using natural ways of breathing, we start to experience what he calls perceptual freedom. Breathing healthily fuels the mindbody with what it needs to attain maximum efficiency, thereby freeing our senses to respond to the actual needs of the moment. This perceptual freedom results in us seeing reality in new ways with new possibilities, freeing us from the locks and chains of prior conditioning and outdated patterns.

To open and free one's breath is to open and free one's mind and perceptions of the surrounding world. Since perception is what creates our experience of reality, by breathing in a healthy way we can change our entire experience of life, from an experience of fear to one of natural health and joy. Truly, each breath is the breath of life. Breathe fully. Notice how you feel. Be in the now.

See simplicity in the complicated.
Achieve greatness in little things.
In the universe the difficult things are done as if they are easy.
In the universe, great acts are made up of small deeds.
The sage does not attempt anything very big, and thus achieves
greatness.
—*Lao Tzu, Tao Te Ching*

In about four months I could paddle out to the lineup, sit on my surfboard without falling off, paddle into a wave using my arms instead of pushing off the bottom with my feet like I did when I first started, and stand up and ride a wave in to shore . . . sometimes. I felt as if I had really accomplished something with my summer. I'm still proud of myself for taking those first terrifying baby steps out of my comfort zone. I'm also grateful to my friend Mersea, who continued to surf with me, give me pointers, loan me surfboards, and offer emotional support.

Then the bigger surf of fall and winter started to roll in, my fear often kept me out of the water. Even when I went out on small days, I wasn't willing to paddle out without other surfers nearby in the water. But I was willing to go without Mersea now. For reasons that defy logic, I felt safer in the lineup with other surfers near me. I kept my distance, though, as I knew I couldn't control my surfboard yet and I didn't want to be in anyone's way. I felt good about what I'd accomplished, but I still had this intense fear thing going on all the time. Breath work certainly improved my control of the fear, but sheer terror was still a major part of my surfing experience. Each time I ventured out into the ocean I had to slowly walk in while focusing on breathing evenly. I never rushed into the water. It usually took me ten minutes of just wading and adjusting to the fact that I was out there before I could lie on the board and paddle out deeper to where the waves were breaking.

Now that I was able to sit there, beyond where the waves break, and float without always falling off the board while the waves rolled through, a different face of my fear showed itself: sharks. My rational mind had come to understand that with a full-body, lifesaving flotation device strapped to my leg, the water could not suck me under. But most surfers who get bit by sharks get bit in the lower leg or foot while sitting on their boards in the lineup. So now this fear was predominant in my mind when bobbing up and down on the ocean surface like a fishing lure, my legs hanging into the water, mimicking the shadowy silhouette of a seal meal to any toothy predators below.

Sometimes I would get spooked out there and have to paddle in to shore just because I thought I saw a menacing shape or fin in the water nearby. Sometimes, when doing surf patrol, if I spotted what I thought might be a fin, I would wait a while, knowing the toothy predators were always moving on, searching for prey. When I first started my standing in the shallows, doing breath work, the thought of sharks did occur to me, but not as strongly as it did now that my vulnerable legs were dangling into the oceanic depths. Very few surfers get bit in the central Florida region, and usually these rare incidents result not in death or dismemberment, but in a scratch or gouge on the lower leg or foot; sometimes, actual bite marks. I didn't personally know anyone, and still don't, who had been bitten by a shark, but this fact didn't calm my irrational fears here, outside my comfort zone.

It wasn't until I had been surfing for three or four years that I had a bona fide shark encounter, but no injury. I was with Mersea when she got a toothy scratch on her hand. It was remarkable. I knew sharks migrated north along this stretch of Atlantic coast every spring. I had witnessed it firsthand the year before.

I had been standing on the boardwalk, looking out at the perfect, beautiful, clear swells, and seeing literally hundreds of small sharks in one enormous school. The sight was visually captivating. I'd never seen anything like it. Scores of beachgoers were taking pictures, and there were a few experienced, dedicated surfers out in the perfect waist-high waves surfing with hundreds of sharks, but very few. Most of us were on the beach or boardwalk, with everyone else just watching the graceful silhouette of a beautiful, flowing, unified school, clearly visible through the shoulder-high waves as the morning sun shone behind them toward the shore. It was breathtaking.

One of the brave surfers out that day rode a wave in and made his way back to shore. He received a cheering hoot and applause from the crowd as he walked up the boardwalk with his shortboard under his arm. He said he was scared and that's why he had only caught a few waves before coming back in. He nervously confirmed that he'd had a couple of close encounters out there. He was quite obviously relieved to be out of the water, unharmed.

It was this same migrating school of sharks that I unknowingly paddled into with Mersea. On a day of wandering cloud cover we loaded our longboards into her Chevy van and drove about an hour south down the coast toward Sebastian Inlet. Sebastian Inlet has a reputation for being a great surf spot. Several surf competitions are held there yearly. There is a state park at the mouth of the inlet where everyone must pay to get to the beach. So Mersea drove to an undesignated fee-free spot just half a mile north of the inlet. It was a place she had surfed often in the past, but I never had. I was intimidated by the reputation of the waves in this area, and more than a little nervous.

Checking from the boardwalk, the surf looked fun: one- to two-foot waves with only a slight chop on the water. We got our boards and paddled out. We didn't get far, about twenty feet off shore, when I noticed a lot of fish in the water below. This immediately freaked me out because they weren't small fish. They were torpedo shaped, like most predator fish, and two- to three-feet long. My mind immediately went to the migrating sharks I had seen the year before. Today the skies were cloudy, and the shadows made it difficult to see into the dark Atlantic waters, but those shapes carpeting the ocean below me looked like a school of migrating sharks.

I yelled to Mersea, "Are those sharks down there?" A calm but terrifying reply of "Yeah, I think so" came back to me. I instantly turned around and paddled back to the safety of the sandy beach. Mersea, on the other hand, seemed undaunted. She didn't turn, pause, or hesitate in any way. She just kept paddling out. From the safety of the shore I continued to watch her thirty- to forty-minute solo surf session. Mersea's fear control was beyond my current capability. What I didn't understand at the time was that she didn't have to control her fear; she simply didn't have any.

She was cautious, though. She kept her limbs pulled up on the board while she lay flat on top of it waiting for waves, instead of sitting with her legs hanging down. She didn't let herself fall off the board into the water either. Not once. This was a skill that took me years to begin learning. She simply turned out of the wave she was riding, back toward the ocean, and went from standing to lying flat on the board and paddled back out for another ride, never getting wet. I saw her constantly scanning all around and into the water, several times pulling her arms up quickly onto the board when paddling back out. Then she'd wait a moment or two, looking into the water, before putting her arms back in to continue paddling.

When she returned to the beach after this short, solitary session, she was exhilarated. She immediately showed me the back of her right hand. It bore a couple of long, shallow scratches from her wrist down toward her fingers. When paddling back out for the last wave she caught, the large school moving through had come up to the surface of the ocean instead of remaining a few feet below, where it had been. As she was lying on her surfboard paddling, reaching forward to plunge her arm into the water for another stroke, a small shark slid up on the surfboard in front of her. With its teeth chomping at her, she instinctively reached out to keep its biting jaws from sliding into her face. At the same time, it slid closer and her hand went into its mouth. Quick as lightning, she pulled back as its toothy jaws were closing. She had suffered a long scrape by its teeth down the back of her retreating hand, but that's all. And that's exactly what the back of her hand looked like: four shallow lines running from the wrist to the first knuckles. The scrapes were deeper toward the wrist, where the teeth first touched her but did not break the skin. She was laughing hysterically the whole time she told me the story. She knew how to Face Everything And Rise.

Mersea understood that this was an isolated opportunity to see an amazing natural event up close and firsthand. She also had enough water experience that she felt she could handle herself in the given conditions. When those conditions became more dangerous, with the sharks near the surface, she came back to shore. She said she didn't blame me one bit for not paddling out with her. She recognized that few people would have. No one else was in the water that day, no one at all, not even ankle wading. Mersea saw that most people, herself included, put limits on our experience of life because of our unfounded fears. Surfing was slowly starting to teach me that too.

She didn't get bit, she could handle the situation given her level of experience, and it was a rare incident. I had now been an eyewitness to people paddling into a huge school of sharks, surfing with them, and returning unharmed on two separate occasions. The fear was irrational, though, and didn't bend to the logic of statistics or even what my own eyes saw. Each time I sat on the surfboard, I envisioned sharks swimming up out of the depths (only ten to fifteen feet deep) and biting into and cutting off my whole thigh. I had a challenging time controlling these thoughts. The visceral visual imagery I experienced was like none I had ever encountered before or since. I blame *Jaws*.

Weapons are instruments of fear; all creatures hate them.
Therefore, followers of Tao never use them.
—Lao Tzu, Tao Te Ching

A re you afraid of sharks? Why? Have you or has anyone you know ever been bitten by one? Chances are you answered no. Of course, few will answer yes. Out of the sheer number of people who go into the ocean, a shark biting a human is an exceptionally rare occurrence. In the United States, there's an average of thirteen to sixteen shark bites per year, usually only one resulting in death. By comparison, in 2016 over thirty-seven thousand people were killed in automobile accidents. Despite this fact, people fear sharks, not cars. Why is that? It's not rational, it has no basis in fact, but somehow it holds tight to us, keeping us from pursuing some of our heart's deepest desires.

In a nonscientific, random survey of my fellow beachgoers one day, I asked everyone I saw (totaling thirty to fifty people) if they'd ever tried surfing. A lot of the kids said yes and that they loved it; fear had yet to set into their young lives. Some of the kids said no because their parents wouldn't let them; someone else's fear was controlling and limiting them. Of the adults, only six said they had tried it. Of those six, five had given up, stating it was too hard, "too much work." Of the adults who said they hadn't tried surfing (most of those surveyed), the reason they ALL gave was fear of sharks.

Jaws ruined the ocean for millions around the world when it first came out. When I was seven and saw it on the big screen, it made me afraid, and that fear stayed with me. As if that weren't enough, sequels of ocean terror soon followed, reinstating the unfounded fear of sharks. Spin-offs continue to this day. Unfortunately, most of these shark terror movies come out in the summer, when most people go to the beach. Artists, particularly those who work in mass-media venues, really need to evaluate the emotions they're unleashing on the world. *Jaws* and its like certainly did not create more love and harmony in the world. No, these movies help generate fear. They profit on fear. I realized that by paying to see scary movies like *Jaws*, I was endorsing and escalating fear and stress within my own personal life and within society.

Nowadays it would be difficult to find a person who isn't stressed. Stress has become an unpleasant fact no matter how much we might attempt to avoid it. Stress and fear have remarkably similar effects on our overall physical health, not to mention our mental health. If my fear of the water hadn't existed and I had partaken of the water parties of my youth, I would have grown up a vastly different person. I would have started surfing at a much younger age than forty if it weren't for this manufactured fear.

If you believe some of your fear has been created by the media you're exposed to, do yourself a huge health favor and stop exposing yourself to that media. There are so many examples of stress generated by media that it's not hard to find one that might be infiltrating your life and damaging your health. It's paying to be scared by horror movies. It's watching the terror-filled nightly news before bed. I used to listen to the news every morning when I got ready for work until I realized how it stressed me out at the very start of my day. So I turned it off, and my day was less stressful. We are buying violent video games, downloading rage-filled music, and viewing violent art. By paying money for the like we are encouraging more stress in our already-stress-dominated world. I started to see that the choice of how my world turns out is mine: expose myself to fear or expose myself to harmony. If I want my world to be peaceful and healthy, I will no longer pay to support violence and fear, whether it comes from games, news, movies, books, politicians, music, or art.

As a forty-year-old grom, scared out of my mind, bobbing up and down on a piece of foam at the mercy of the ocean, I understood that this shark fear was a contrived fear, a false fear: False Evidence Appearing Real. I understood that the haunting images in *Jaws* that I had been exposed to at an incredibly youthful age were not the whole truth. But the images of fear had embedded themselves into my not fully formed young brain as reality. My rational mind also understood that to go with the flow of the ocean, to surf, I had to relax despite the fear. My rational mind comprehended this and could formulate how to do it: get control of my fear breathing, then get control of my trembling-in-fear body. As renowned master B. K. S. Iyengar has said, "Regulate the breathing and thereby control the mind."

While my precious legs dangled off the surfboard bobbing up and down like a fishing lure, regulating my breath was difficult enough, but I also had to get control of the quivers of fear that ran through my body. For this I used the Progressive Scientific Relaxation Technique. I had learned it in Supreme Science qigong training. Progressively scan the whole body, and focus on each individual part to get it to relax. Starting at my vulnerable feet, I focused my mind on relaxing and letting go, using the least possible muscular effort to let them hang in the water. Then the ankles letting go, the calves and shins, the knees loosening and opening more as the quads and hamstrings released excess tension. From there I progressively took my mind (my *yi*, or intention) to the next body part and envisioned the muscles releasing their tension until I had worked all the way up through my jaw, forehead, and face. The entire process took three to five minutes.

While I sat terrified on the surfboard after paddling out, my logical mind could easily run this sequence through a full-body scan from feet to head. This progressive relaxation technique kept my body from trembling, which it continued to do for a few years into surfing. At the same time, my rational mind was busy calming my breath so there was little attention to give to the irrational shark anxiety. It took time, but with patience and persistence, the shark dread gradually slipped further into the recesses of my mind. As this happened, my technical skills on the surfboard improved. It was as though letting go of the fear a bit allowed my body to flow in better harmony with its surroundings.

I was starting to understand that surfing was teaching me the same lessons as tai chi practice and the *Tao Te Ching*: when I could let go and get out of my own way, I could easily go with the flow. I had to release my tight grip on what I thought *was*, so that I could flow into a new perception of reality and a new way of being.

While my fear persisted, it was not stopping me anymore and was becoming background noise in my surf experiences instead of the heart of them. Surfing was slowly taking a greater hold on my life, and I was driving south to surf better waves on a regular basis. Moving from the quiet of being out past the break in the ocean to being in wintertime traffic on A1A in the heart of Florida was sometimes tough. People from out of town, usually northeastern states, would often be in a rush, driving too fast even though they weren't sure where they were going. I noticed a lot more horn honking in the increased traffic during Florida's most touristy season: winter. I smelled the traffic more too, not only when I was walking to or from the beach or sitting in my own polluting car, but also drifting out off shore.

It was as though, out in the ocean, my senses were washed clean.

The salt water sure did keep my skin and sinuses clear with a thorough washing with each session. It made sense that I could smell better because of it. My awareness of sound also seemed to extend farther when waiting for waves. The sounds of the seagulls and brown pelicans gliding over the waves became as familiar as the seashell wind chimes on my back porch. I became aware that I heard the sounds from the shore better when I was in front of the breaking waves than when I was sitting behind them. The movement of the waves' energy toward shore seemed to push the sound vibrations of everything taking place on the land away from me, making them seem more distant than they were. My hearing became more sensitive, and just the sounds of being in traffic became disquieting.

I didn't want to be part of that stinky, noisy, polluting, frustrating traffic anymore, so I moved south to the less commercial small town of Satellite Beach, where I found myself driving most often to surf. The waves are more consistent there, and the town is less trashed by those passing through on spring break or vacation. Cocoa Beach is great and has some wonderful attractions. It was the ideal place for me to start confronting my ocean fear since I could casually wade out into the shallow ocean. I still make the short drive on occasion. While Florida's beaches will inevitably be tourist attractions, some places feel more like home than just stops along the way. Satellite Beach is one of those special places.

There's a small reef system that doesn't exist just a few miles to the north or south. The "rocks" in the water draw more fish to the area and create daunting obstacles for fishermen, swimmers, and surfers to navigate. This makes it a much less popular tourist destination than the smooth, sandy bottoms of Daytona, Cocoa, and Miami Beaches. Maybe it's the rocks or the way the coastline is shaped there; maybe it's that the beach hasn't been "restored" as long. Who knows what it is, but the surf is a little more consistent along the three miles of Satellite Beach's shoreline than the more popular areas of the coast.

A small two-bedroom duplex, only a minute's walk to the beach, was available, so I took it and started learning to surf in earnest. Yes, I could now surf a little, but my fear was still there, and I couldn't control what the surfboard did when I was standing on it—or even lying on it sometimes, for that matter. I still had a tough time reading the conditions from shore before heading into the water; and I had to have people around me even if I didn't know them, just so I could paddle out. My updated goal now was to totally overcome my fear of the water and become a decent longboard surfer. Just as with my tai chi journey, the more I learned about surfing, the better I could refine where I wanted it to take me.

Learning to surf and learning tai chi have both taught me similar life lessons. In fact, I'd say, despite having gone to college, traveled extensively, lived off-grid, had several careers, and tried every sport and activity out there, it is tai chi and surfing that have taught me the most about how to live well. They have taught me the lessons of the Tao. At this point, both tai chi and surfing began to take on parallel life-altering roles in my life to an undeniable degree. I reflected that I had started surfing to get rid of fear and tai chi to get rid of rage, and that was just the start of what the two held in common for me.

When I was around twenty-three, I had a severe anger problem. It started as teenage angst and grew from there. Thankfully, the slow-motion martial art meditation of tai chi saved me from my own self-destructive violence and rage. No one in my family was violent. I didn't have any personal experience with violence in my life, but for some reason, when I became mad, I always became enraged and violent. It wasn't until I neared my twenties and started to recognize the outrageous injustice in the world of humanity that my rage became overwhelming. Fortunately, I did not lash out physically at others. I turned my rage on myself and beat myself to pieces. On recurring occasions, I broke my feet, hands, ankles, and wrists kicking and punching things out of sheer rage, all the while failing to see I had a problem.

Then one day, running my own successful business as sole proprietor, I became so angry that I punched and kicked myself right out of work. I had one tremendous fit of rage over a flat tire, which resulted from a lot of nails in the road. I broke my left wrist and my right foot punching and kicking my truck, making it impossible for me to operate my land maintenance business for six weeks. In six weeks, I lost half my clients that had taken me years to gain. In six weeks, even though I hired others to do the physical labor, the three grown men I hired simply couldn't keep up with what I—one small, young, fiery, motivated woman—could do. So I lost money, I lost reputation, and I became depressed. With more time on my hands than I'd ever had as an adult, I moped and then thought about what had happened. Slowly I realized I had to start controlling this anger or it might just kill me in one way or another.

There were no anger management classes back then. The term didn't even exist. I tried a psychologist. It didn't help and was expensive. I tried meditation. Didn't help, I couldn't sit still like that; I was too absorbed with doing. Maybe this moving meditation, this tai chi I'd heard of, would help. So I set about trying to find a teacher. Ha! Florida is still just as conservative as it's always been, and finding a teacher of something as esoteric and foreign as tai chi simply was not an option in 1990. So I went to the cool, funky, purple New Age store I had seen way out on A1A in Indialantic Beach (there was no public Internet yet) where they sold a variety of "alternative" self-help stuff. I lucked out. Tucked in a corner of the book section was a twirling, tall white wire rack with numerous VHS videos of yoga, meditation, and tai chi chuan. There were two options: Yang short form or Yang long form. I was in a hurry. I wanted help now, quickly, ideally within six weeks. I bought the short form tape.

To me, that first lesson felt far from short. It seemed to last an infinite amount of painful, tedious time. The teacher on the video wanted me to stand still with my arms out in front of me for two minutes, to stand, relax, and breathe. Stand still for *two whole minutes*? It was unbelievably torturous to my "be productive, DO something" Western-conditioned mind. But, unable to work now, I had a lot of time on my hands, so I learned to stand still. Then I learned to breathe slowly and deeply. Then I tried to relax while standing still. Then I tried to relax and breathe while moving slowly. *Tried* is the keyword here.

I was astonished how difficult this slow-moving stuff was. I found it frustrating, and often I felt stupid because I couldn't take a step softly or I had a challenging time remembering where to put my hand. I criticized my performance a lot. It was a good video. Learning from VHS was brutal. I had to constantly stop, walk to the machine, stop, rewind, try to find where I was, and then go again. Some days going back and forth to the VCR took me more time than the actual tai chi movement I was learning.

Going back and forth to the VCR was also teaching me patience, something I desperately needed. The tai chi movement was extremely slow. I wasn't used to that. It pushed my patience in ways I hadn't expected. It was challenging, this slow-motion therapy. I liked it. I enjoyed being challenged to grow, even then.

It didn't happen right away. It took me about a year and a half of going through the lessons in that video for hours every single day before I could remember the Yang short form. But I did get there. And that's when the chi magic started to really work. Once I could remember the movements, I was able to focus on relaxing my muscles and using minimal effort: effortless effort. This became my moving meditation: being present in my body moving through space, aware of every step I take, every move I make, and every breath. I was learning how to live in and move my body, which was teaching me how to control myself. If I could make myself practice when I was enraged, the anger dissipated. Even though I was practicing a martial art, I was learning to let go of my violent rage. I was too inexperienced to see the yin and yang of that. Years later, I learned from Bruce Lee that martial arts are more about knowing and controlling ourselves than learning to fight.

After teaching myself this complicated tai chi set, I continued to practice tai chi daily, and I still do today. When I sold my lawn business and traveled for a few years, I studied with several different teachers here and there. I learned a short, modified Wu-style tai chi set and got certified to teach several forms of qigong just because I wanted to learn it in greater depth, not because I wanted to teach it. I didn't have a teacher or mentor, so to speak, as I had studied at various places with several teachers in assorted styles; so my training, though consistent, was a bit eclectic. But I was dedicated to my own personal daily practice even without a teacher, class, or tai chi group. As I practiced every day, no matter where I was living or traveling, my connection to flowing and letting go was very slowly deepening.

Years later, when I moved to Satellite Beach to improve my surfing and resolve my fear, I discovered a true tai chi master and began to study in earnest, pushing myself farther to release my water fear through surfing and pushing myself farther to move effortlessly through tai chi, both challenging goals. Both reminded me of Leonardo da Vinci's words "One can have no smaller or greater mastery than mastery of oneself." I felt in good company.

Surfing with this new rocky reef situation certainly made it more challenging, especially for an awkward, scared forty-something like me. Here, in the rocky waters of Satellite Beach, I could no longer easily and carelessly wade out into the ocean. Trying to spot the underwater barriers by looking for the eddies on the water's surface was near impossible for me at first. Before walking into the water, I'd look and look, trying to spot the underwater rocks, only to get trapped by an unseen waist-high wall of towering, algae-covered rock. I had to learn a lot to surf there. The hidden rocks left me with a lot of cuts and scrapes and reef rash I obtained in the learning process. It is only through failure that we begin to succeed.

Within a few months, Mersea and I had this beach wired. We knew the most dangerous rocks were big ledges closer to the shoreline that had big holes where legs and feet could get caught. We knew where the larger, deeper outcroppings were that jacked up the wave to create a better break off the flat, sandy bottom surrounding it. We learned quickly that low-tide surf was much more dangerous, as the rocks were more exposed and often impossible to float or paddle over. Sometimes the low-tide waves would break and throw an unprepared surfer directly onto a big, barnacled, table-like rock with brutal results. I got hurt numerous times in super-shallow water with small waves. In fact, lots of people did and still do there, not just me. Even Mersea, with all of her water skills and knowledge, would occasionally come out from a session with a big, bloody gash on her shin from having stumbled into a hidden, underwater rock.

Navigating these new rocky waters was certainly a distraction to my fear, even though the fear persisted. Learning how to paddle over, through, and around these obstacles also made me stronger and a much better paddler. Before surfing in Cocoa Beach, I had been walking out to where the waves broke. Now I had to paddle a lot more. In the beginning, my arms would be so tired from just a ninety-minute surf session that I could not lift them for several hours. Several times I dropped fragile surfboards on the hard, unforgiving asphalt as I ran back home across A1A. Surfing here was making me a fitter forty-something.

My new tai chi *shifu* (*shi* = to be, *fu* = expert), Grand Master Jeff Cook, helped with fitness as well. Up until then, all of my tai chi and qigong training had been in very soft, yin, yielding styles of movement. Now I had a teacher who was a master of several martial arts, not just a gentle tai chi master. Shifu Cook is extremely hard-core. He enjoys it when he has an opportunity to fight. He does not look for a fight, but if a fight should come and pressure him, he truly delights in getting to utilize his well-honed skills.

His style of tai chi was new to me. Even though anyone could do the exercises, they were not presented as something for old ladies or the infirm, as is often the stereotyped image of tai chi. Instead, tai chi and qigong were presented as the traditional training for fighters and warriors. His is an old style, predating the forms within the more common five-family system of classification. The warm-up qigong set was more strenuous than I ever knew qigong could be. The centuries-old *yi jin ching* practice balances strength of muscles with their softness. It is a complex qigong practice designed to balance mind, body, and spirit, combining focused breath work, symmetrical isometric training, balance, and visualization techniques.

With *yi jin ching* we strengthen against ourselves in balance and symmetry. In so doing we find our own powerful, individual center of balance. Here we avoid any possibility of harming ourselves, as can sometimes happen when strengthening against an outside force like weights. Instead, we use our bodies as the resistance, fulcrum, and power to strengthen ourselves from within. In *yi jin ching*, as in life, our breath and our will, or *yi*, drives it all. Typically, qigong and tai chi practices mimic the journey of life itself by beginning with an inhale and ending on an exhale. In between we learn how to control ourselves, to be responsible for our mindbody.

I could feel the practice making me stronger, more centered, and giving me energy in a way I never felt from any other exercise. I was hooked from the start on this fifth-century mindbody training. When it comes to exercise, I had difficulty sticking to Western-style workouts. After a few months, the workouts would become rote and boring. Tai chi workouts have always kept my attention.

Up to this point, tai chi had taught me how to relax my muscles and let go. Now I was learning to use this relaxation to release residual tension after concentrated muscular effort. I was learning to balance my yin with yang. I was learning the middle way, the way of balance, the natural way of the Tao.

Look, it cannot be seen—it is beyond form.
Listen, it cannot be heard—it is beyond sound.
Grasp, it cannot be held—it is intangible.
It returns to nothingness.
The form of the formless.
The image of the imageless.
It is called indefinable and beyond imagination.
—Lao Tzu, *Tao Te Ching*

To practice qigong and tai chi at sunrise on the beach every day was a blessing and a privilege. I was profoundly grateful, and I could see how it was altering my perception of myself and the world around me. My life was becoming more about the beach and the ebb and flow of the tides than I had ever expected. When I started reading Lao Tzu's *Tao Te Ching* on the advice of Shifu Cook, I started to become completely immersed in a world that flows and morphs continuously, existing beyond the confines of rigid, unfluctuating, man-made systems. I was learning not just the rhythms of the surf and of breathing and movement, but also the cyclical flow of relationships, societies, stars, galaxies, and empires, and how it truly is all Tao. I was starting to understand surfing in terms of Tao, and I was understanding some of the Tao because of surfing.

Most people are familiar with the spectacle of surfing even if they've never been to the beach. The appealing, fluid, graceful images of surfing can be seen in many visual mass-media marketing campaigns. Surfing is used to sell beer, cars, and insurance, and its image alone carries a sense of a relaxed, easy, flowing lifestyle. So what is all this Tao stuff I keep talking about? Good question. As the fifth-century Taoist master Lao Tzu told us at the start, "The Tao that can be told is not the eternal Tao." True. Yet to understand Tao and to understand surfing's relationship to Tao, we must have a general understanding of the word *Tao*.

The typical Western translation of *Tao* (pronounced "dow") is "the Way." So, the Tao is the Way. I just love saying that! It took me many years to even begin to comprehend what that means, and I'm still learning it. The Chinese character for *Tao* is composed of two parts: the top character represents a head, and the bottom character represents a path or way. So, a more comprehensive understanding of Tao would be that it is a path one follows with purposeful choices rather than with feet, using wisdom instead of force, will instead of strength.

Yet the Tao is more than the path, it is also the unfolding of the path, and to some it can seem godlike. While Taoism can connect us to the Tao and help create "wholeness," leaving us feeling (w)holy and spiritual, it is not a religion. Taoism is a philosophy that promotes living with harmony according to the balanced ways of nature, walking our path through life in balance. In Taoism, creation and creator are the same, as all is one within Tao. We can see this truth in neuroscience, discovering that we can create our physical reality through our mental reality. The well-known symbol of Tao is the black-and-white balanced, swooping circle that shows the relationship between yin and yang. The circle contains the two aspects of all there is in our world, intermingling with and transforming each other.

Most people know what a surfer is, but what then is a Taoist? As

I understand it, from a conglomeration of various sources over many years, a Taoist is one who studies the ways of nature using observation and experimentation and then uses the knowledge gained to live in natural harmony. Because Tao is evident in the ways of nature, studying natural laws, cycles, and rhythms can give insight to the nature of Tao. Many masters live immersed in nature far away from the "noise of men" to observe the cycles and rhythms of the natural world more easily.

Some people mistakenly think Taoism is a religion and that practicing it will conflict with their religious beliefs. While there is a small church devoted to a sect of Taoism, overall it is not considered a religion, as no one is worshiped, there is no set-forth doctrine to follow to be considered a Taoist, and the ways of nature are universal to all life, not just one group of believers. No faith is required to see what is. Many people all over the world consider themselves both Taoist and, say, Catholic, Buddhist, Muslim, or even atheist, as the ways of nature are universal to all, regardless of culture, religion, race, or any other separationist grouping. Therefore, it is easy to see Tao in the natural laws of the surf, regardless of your spiritual beliefs.

Most dedicated surfers would agree that surfing has a very spiritual side not at all associated with religion. In fact, surfing might border on being religious to some surfers in their sheer devotion to it. It is the surfer's full immersion in the Sea of Chi, the Tao of it all, the ways of nature, that brings him in contact with something more than just the physical reality of the sport. The surfer connects to nature through all the physical senses—touch, taste, sight, smell, and sound—on a plane that is deeper than the landlocked two-dimensional life. This purposeful full-sensory immersion in the elemental nature of being human can thrust the surfer, just as it does the Big Kahuna, medicine man, or master, into contact with the unified field, bringing on the euphoric, often spiritual experience.

The surfer studies the ways of nature and, through years of experimentation with a surfboard, learns to move in harmony with the wave, which is the energy of heaven and earth combined. So, to become a surfer is, at some level, to become a Taoist. Both Taoist and surfer would agree that it takes true skill to simply relax and go with the flow. Both would agree that effortless effort does not come easily, which is why so few attain it. Both would also agree that by learning their art, they've learned how to live in better harmony with nature.

In the study of Taoism, one observes both nature and many texts, most prominent of which is Lao Tzu's *Tao Te Ching*. When recommending it to me, Shifu Cook said, "It's the only book you need to read about tai chi and what we practice." I thought it would be a technical book on movement and breathing, not a book of esoteric poetry. There are many translations of this ancient work at the heart of Taoism. In fact, it's only outnumbered in translations by the Bible. Just as one cannot read the Bible cover to cover like a novel and get it all, one cannot read the *Tao Te Ching* in one sitting and comprehend it fully. Through years of study, its layered meanings unfold.

In addition to studying the *Tao Te Ching* and observing nature, meditation is also used in the Taoist way. Finally, the most challenging path to learn the Tao is to study tai chi chuan (*tai* = great, *chi* = breath, *chuan* = striking part of fist), or the "grand ultimate exercise." Little did I know when I started that one can't take a few tai chi classes and then have it, even though I was looking for a quick fix when I turned to tai chi. Like the movements of the practice itself, and like surfing, to learn tai chi takes commitment, patience, and perseverance; these are in fact integral parts of the lessons of the Tao.

First, we learn the choreography, the physical steps and movements that make up the tai chi form, or routine. Then we learn to integrate the tai chi principles of efficient movement. Synchronizing our breathing with our movements is also an important aspect of tai chi practice. Finally, we begin to meld all the above and recognize how the practice of tai chi affects energy (or chi) flow in the mindbody. If a practitioner is so inclined, he may also learn the martial art application of the movements in the tai chi form. There's quite a bit more to it than just moving slowly.

To learn tai chi is much like peeling an onion: at first, we only see the outside layer, but by peeling back the layers we can see that it is the core that expands and holds the layers together. By learning this slow tai chi dance we start to see how our energy and whole being is affected by how we choose to move and breathe, and eventually it teaches us how to flow effortlessly through the challenges of life, how to keep our center when the world around us is swirling.

The same can be said of surfing. Like the challenging physical study of tai chi, learning to surf follows a similar process: understand the basic moves, integrate the principles of fluid movement, observe the flow of energy in the water/wave, learn to regulate one's breathing in the water, then refine and integrate all of the above into what looks like an effort-less dance between ocean and surfer. Often in the process, the surfer finds herself devoted to surfing, as though it were a religion, just like tai chi and Taoism. But effortless effort is not easy to attain on land and even more challenging on water.

The surfer uses her wisdom to study the ways of the water and move flowingly in harmony with that ever-morphing energy. Surfing is a path undertaken with one's head through a progression of purposeful choices and followed through on with the courage of the heart. Surfing is both an activity and a lifestyle, as it is an actual journey to surf. To simply take a surfboard to the beach a time or two and get in the water with it is one thing. But to really learn to surf is truly a journey that becomes a way of life.

To surf even just once, a series of sometimes complex choices is in-volved. Even before the would-be surfer hits the water, a lot must take place to get there: procuring a surfboard and a wetsuit, having a way to get the board to the beach, planning the trip, going to the beach, and if there are good waves, then trying to surf. It's a series of choices that must take place before one ever drops into the wave and rides it. Most spectators only equate surfing to the actual riding of the wave, but it is much more than just this one flowing action.

After all the planning and preparation is accomplished and one does finally engage the water, there are crucial decisions made there, some of which require courage: facing a big overhead onslaught of whitewash can be overwhelming if you're not used to it. I quickly learned that more courage is required to simply stand up on the surfboard. When you catch the wave on your stomach, you and your board hopefully will start to go down the face of the wave with it breaking just slightly behind you. This is where you jump up onto your feet to maneuver the board on the wave. In my fearful reality, what was taking place was that I had to force myself to jump to my feet at the very moment I wanted to get down because I was falling down the face of the wave with an avalanche of water galloping down on top of me like a powerful herd of wild horses stampeding behind me. The last thing I wanted to do was jump to my feet. It went against every primal idea of self-preservation that was in me. It took more courage than I had ever imagined.

And the whole while I'm wondering: Do I try to take this wave, or will the next one be better? If I take off now, will I crash into the person next to me, who is also trying to catch the wave? Which way do I go so I don't slam into a rock? And then the ultimate decision: Do I continue to do this after today? Was it worth it? Or do I get rid of this stupid, hard-to-transport surfboard and move on to the next thing? As the surfer progresses, the decisions become more technical: Is the current too strong to paddle out today? Can I make a drop in that steep with a nine-foot surfboard? These choices don't end because the waves and conditions are never the same; they are constantly shifting. Surfing is a journey into an entire lifestyle that one arrives at only through a series of choices over years. It is done with mindful purpose and intention, not just by wandering along a well-worn, easy, comfortable path.

Watching the strength and power of professional surfers in contest conditions, some believe that surfing is a way of the body more than the mind. Yet like the onion, Tao, tai chi, and surfing are not what they appear to be on their surfaces. Yes, surfing is a physical act that requires physical effort, making it a body activity. Yet if surfing were all about the strength of the body, how is it that small children can paddle out into large overhead waves that knock grown men off their feet? Is it the strength of the ten-year-old's body that propels her forward through the oncoming force of the white water? To a certain degree, yes, of course there has to be some physical effort involved, but more important than muscling through the resistance of whitewash when it comes head-on is understanding the flow of the energy and using the hydrodynamic laws of motion to offer the least possible resistance, letting the wave pass by and then paddle on. This is using one's head and heart (as courage is required to face a head-on rush of powerful energy), which in Chinese medicine are united together in a healthy person.

Neither I nor the ten-year-old grom had studied hydrodynamics and could use engineering language to describe the paddle-out process. More than likely though, the ten-year-old could describe the process in surf lingo, which is quite complex, just as hydrodynamics is complex. But if that grom can paddle out, then she's learned from observation and experimentation to understand the movement of water and the best way to let the oncoming force of it pass by so she's not struggling against the whitewash. She has learned to just relax, let go, and allow the flow to happen in its due course. She is learning the Tao.

But there's a big "if" involved. Most novices won't make it past the learning stage, especially if they're adults when they start. It is not easy to learn effortless effort in paddling out past breaking surf. In fact, in my nonstatistical survey of adults on my beach, of the few who had tried surfing as adults, about 99 percent said they gave it up because it was "way too hard." But if that were true, that surfing is physically grueling and only for the athletically supreme, then how do sixty-pound kids paddle out? Or beer-bellied, roly-poly Jimmy Buffet wannabes— how do they paddle out? Or how did a small, 124-pound, five-foot-six woman like professional surfer Maya Gabeira break the women's world record and surf a giant sixty-foot wave? Strength does play a part in surviving extreme big-wave surfing, but purposeful, mindful choices are more useful in walking the path effectively.

In life it is the same: we must use our bodies to propel us physically through the journey, but our choices determine what kind of journey that life is. Surfing, like tai chi, requires patience, dedication, and a willingness to dive into something much larger than ourselves, to let go into the flow of life itself.

Accept disgrace willingly.
Accept misfortune as the human condition.
—*Lao Tzu, Tao Te Ching*

No matter how athletic you are, the ocean is stronger, faster, and more in control. Learning to surf is truly humbling. Inevitably the new surfer will be humiliated in the learning process. Some groms quit simply because they "lose face," as the Chinese say, especially older newbies like me who as adults have a firmly established sense of self-identity. Kids' egos are still forming and don't get bruised as easily from failure. Thank goodness, or we humans might never learn to walk!

One humiliating incident stands out from my first summer of surf in Cocoa Beach. It happened at the extremely popular Lori Wilson Park. I had been surfing three to four months. I could now paddle out, catch a wave, shakily stand up, and maintain my balance for more than five seconds. That's about all my months of physically draining efforts had advanced me. The surf was small that day, a requirement for me at this point in the journey. Mersea and I were soaking in the windless, golden sun along with lots of other beachgoers that day. Quite a few small kids were in the water too, as the conditions were so gentle.

My arms feeling like noodles after a nice, long session, I was heading back in to shore. I felt good about my surfing that day, but I was ready for a break. I rode my longboard into shore on my belly until I got in about eight-inch-deep water, where I promptly got humiliated by the ocean. When I tried to stand up I simply couldn't. For some reason, every time I tried to put my feet down in the sand, I fell over. I fell over on my butt. I fell over on my knees. I fell over and busted my head on my surfboard so hard that I saw stars and sat down hard in the water, flat on my behind, making a big splash. After just sitting there a moment, I shook it off and managed to walk onto the beach, but noticed that practically everyone basking in the sun was staring at me. I went from feeling good about my session to being totally humiliated in a matter of seconds.

Fortunately (some might say unfortunately), every surfer who sticks with it will eventually be humiliated by the ocean. I now cherish this about surfing. Back when I got thrown down repeatedly as a grom, it would hurt my pride. Now, I sometimes purposely go out when conditions are rough just so I can get tossed by the ocean, laughing all the way. I now understand why people boogie board into cataclysmic wave conditions like the famous Wedge in Newport Beach, California, or Sandy Beach on Oahu, Hawaii. In both places the waves jack up quickly to build thick, towering walls of heavy water in milliseconds, creating fast-,falling avalanches of dense salt water in just a few short feet.

These treacherous conditions attract thousands of thrill seekers, who plunge in to take advantage of steep, fast drops into the wave. YouTube videos abound of watery mayhem as people get flipped, slammed, barrel-rolled, thrown, shoved, tossed, grounded, pretzeled, and abused by these powerful near-shore waves. When I first witnessed this in person, I was astounded that anyone could walk away from the pounding unscathed let alone laughing and smiling. But with enough experience in the water, I've come to understand how to take a beating gracefully and gratefully by simply relaxing and letting go.

In fact, my perspective has changed entirely. Now I see it as an ocean massage instead of an ocean beating. Usually I can come out of it laughing and smiling even though the ocean's tossed me around like a rag doll. When the forceful water rushes over my relaxed limbs, it's strong enough to move my muscles, causing a rolling, undulating, massage-like effect. The ocean is kneading and rolling my muscles while at the same time detoxifying and flushing the toxins out of my body. While my muscles are getting worked over and forcefully massaged by the huge hands of the ocean waves, the salt water is pulling biotoxins out of my skin through diffusion. Just like in a human-given massage, I must relax and not tighten up so the therapist's work is more effective. As with most things healing, I must consciously relax and voluntarily release my muscular tension so that the magic of the healing can take place.

If I hold on tightly, bracing for impact from the oncoming wave, then it does become a beating. If I can let go and allow it to wash over me and simply roll with its force, it is a salty, healing massage. After even a short ocean massage session I am revived, refreshed, and rejuvenated. I am healed by the ocean. I have produced nothing, paid no one, left no trace, and powerful healing of my mindbody has taken place. I walk away barefoot, smiling and laughing, dripping with salty joy and the release from burden. All of my senses are fully cleansed and satisfied: touch, smell, taste, hearing, sight. I return to my work and life with renewed perspective.

While seeking the ocean beating/massage isn't for everyone, all who venture in regardless of conditions will eventually learn the humbleness taught by the power and grandeur of the sea. To continue entering the water, despite the embarrassment, danger, fear, and sheer physicality of it, doesn't make sense to those who never step out of their comfort zones. Because some people don't give themselves opportunities to grow, their courage and self-confidence rarely has an opportunity to develop and fully shine. A dedicated surfer's courage is pushed with each new wave. There is no rote repetition in surfing, like hitting in a batting cage. Each wave is different; a surfer must be present, or the wipeout becomes their reality.

Even with all the danger, fear, humiliation, and physical and mental hardships of surfing, it's worth every single bit of it. The high is insanely better than the low. In fact, the feeling is so good that surfers have given the euphoria from surfing its own name: stoke. To be stoked means you are high on surfing. To have stoke means your energy is elevated. To get stoked means your chi is rising. Yes, there's nothing quite like the surf stoke. The high of a great wave, even just one great ride, can last not only all day but all week! It can make the sting of a nasty divorce go away; the loss felt from a departed love one lessens. A horrible, stressful work week can simply disappear when riding the energy of the cosmos. That high can even go on to revitalize you months and sometimes even years later, or I should say the memory of that ride can reach you even beyond the now. Just to recall a perfectly executed turn or a nice drop-in from a past session while you're in the middle of a stressful day can calm the spirit. It has for me.

When you think about it, to surf is to ride the energy of the cosmos. I think the stoke comes from not just riding but absorbing the energy of heaven and earth. To understand this better, let's consider how a wave is formed. The energy of the sun causes wind in our atmosphere to blow over the waters of the earth, which makes that water move. That chi/energy movement within the water is often enhanced by the pull of the moon and/or surface winds. When the cosmic chi energy is moving through the water toward land, the bottom surface eventually becomes shallower and the moving energy has nowhere to go but up. This forms the breaking, surfable wave. I think of it as the energy of the cosmos combining with the energy of the earth, and I am standing right at the height of all this power on my surfboard. I'm in the curl, or spiral, of all this galactic chi.

This is where the absorption-of-energy part comes in. In the study of tai chi, we learn that the *yon quan* acupuncture points on the balls of the feet not only connect us to the earth but also draw chi, or energy, into the physical body. This point is often called the Bubbling Well because of the feeling a practitioner might get in this part of the foot when earth energy is pouring into the body through this highly receptive point, like energy bubbling up into the foot. This point is also where we can find balance with the foot planted on a surfboard, or the ground, or when we need to stand on our toes. So, the surfer is standing right on top of the most powerful part of the wave on one of the most energy-receptive parts of the body. The surfer is standing there, rooted down into the board, while the energy of the cosmos is rolling like a foaming mountain right beneath the Bubbling Well point. I believe part of the surf stoke is the chi of the cosmos coming into the surfer through the Bubbling Well acupuncture point. This causes the stoke, the chi fire, the energy high. This galactic energy rush is so powerful that extreme big-wave surfers are willing to risk their lives to get it.

This cosmic rush of energy can also be experienced through some qigong practices. I've experienced a similar type of energy rush, or stoke, with powerful qigong breathing exercises or simply practicing in a large group. It's a feeling that is tangible but indefinable, a surge of energy felt throughout the body that leaves the mind open and energy renewed. It's a palpable high that is crisp and clean with no bad side effects like the synthetic euphoria from drugs. Instead there's a restored sense of hope and an overwhelming experience of love for the world. This energy-awakening experience from qigong and tai chi did not come quickly or easily for me. Breath work, like surfing, was humbling at first when I realized how little control I had over my mind and breath, before I learned qigong breathing.

As I progressed in learning how to breathe mindfully, I gradually recognized how learning to breathe healed all aspects of my life. I began to recognize things within my own breathing patterns that were unhealthy, and I consciously tried to change those things. I knew from qigong classes and reading that a healthy breath, one that promotes better health in the mindbody, is one where there is no pause or stagnation, where the cycle of "breathe in, breathe out" is continuous with no holding of the breath anywhere. I observed that I usually held my breath when exerting even a small amount of physical effort in daily life. I noticed that I usually held my breath in the shower. I wondered if this somehow related to my intense, primal fear of water.

Now that I was recognizing unhealthy breathing patterns within myself, I was consciously trying to change them. When I caught myself holding my breath in the shower for instance, I made sure I stayed focused on not stopping the breath for the remainder of my time there. I started to notice that after showering now, I felt more refreshed. My past feeling that I had to rush, put on my clothes, and move on to doing the next thing was starting to dissipate. I began to see the shower as more than just getting rid of dirt, as an actual cleansing that was healing. I took more time to savor the simple joy of having hot water and indoor plumbing, which hasn't always been the case in my life. Slowly, I was beginning to respect water.

Controlling the breath isn't really the goal in breath-work exercises. Conditioning the breath is. Just like any other muscular system in the body, breathing can be made better through exercise. I rationalized that since my fear and breathing seemed to be related to each other, if I could control the breathing a little, I should be able to control the fear. We certainly shouldn't be trying to control our breathing all the time, but in my case, the conditioning worked for my goal.

As I let go of old breath-holding patterns, I noticed that my life changed as well. My perception seemed to widen a little in its scope. As my breath expanded, so did how I viewed the world around me. I began to take things like someone flipping me off in traffic less personally. I saw that I didn't have to absorb the energy of that driver's difficult day; I could let it roll right past me like a wave I didn't want to catch. I was feeling a lot more self-confident and less lonely. I was still alone in my life, but somehow it didn't seem to matter anymore. My experience of myself as a conscious entity seemed to expand along with my loosening breath. As Dennis Lewis puts it, "As our breath expands into hitherto unconscious parts of ourselves—our attitudes and emotions start to change, and our self-image begins to release its stranglehold on our lives."

It was like I had let go of a fear pattern in my breathing and this released a fear pattern in my life. For the first time in my life I could "breathe easy." Holding the breath is most definitely a fear pattern. When we get startled or scared, we tense our muscles and hold or shorten our breath, preparing for what may come next. Is there danger? Do I need to run? Do I need to fight? I'm ready, braced for impact, and my adrenaline is pumping! This is something we unconsciously learn first as babies when startled by loud, unfamiliar noises. Then, over time, we may learn to hold the breath any time we're stressed. Stress and fear do go together. They have remarkably similar chemical and emotional effects on us.

I don't know about you, but I have a lot more stress in my stress-free life than I ever imagined possible. The stress of hearing and being in traffic, Ebola, toxic homes, nuclear weapons, ISIS, genetically modified food, polluted air, Russia, Zika, climate change, artificial intelligence, nuclear threats, overpopulation, drought, fires, hurricanes, deadly flu outbreaks—we do live in incredibly stressful times. Even the sound of cars is stressful, whether you admit it to yourself or not. Just as some sounds create calm, the opposite is true: traffic noise creates discord. I can't imagine anyone would say the sound of traffic is peaceful and calming. And unless you live completely news-free on your own 100 percent organic, engineless island, you're exposed to overwhelming stress every day that the human organism as we know it has never had to deal with before. There's a lot of us who hold our breath a little simply because of the stress and fear that constantly surround us.

We know what a panicked breath is, so what is a healthy breath? From what I've learned over the years, a healthy breath has an equal inhale and exhale; there is no pause or stop in the cycle of in and out. It is not forced but effortless and full, utilizing most of the lungs' capacity. It is slow, ideally five to ten breaths per minute, in and out of the nose, quiet. Once I started to learn this, I was able to see patterns in my own breathing that were way off, and it wasn't always the same patterns. I breathed in different ways in relationship to the emotion of what I was doing. The previous example of holding my breath in the shower was obvious. I also found that I tended to breathe more shallowly when sitting than standing. Since more of my time was spent sitting at a computer, I needed to cultivate a full breath for my brain to work well navigating the digital world. I started using a harder, less comfortable chair that forced me to sit up straighter and therefore be able to breathe with more of my lungs. When I did this, my computer work improved.

The aspect of the healthy breath that still gets me the most is the slowness of it. Five to ten breaths per minute is the range that is considered the healthiest. That is slow. One study I came across even concluded that three to five breaths per minute was the healthiest, as it kept brain-wave patterns steady and consistent. According to the American Respiratory Association, the average rate of respiration for humans is twelve to sixteen breaths per minute, while the average American breathes fifteen to twenty breaths per minute. That's a pretty significant difference from a healthy five to ten breaths every minute.

When I tried to count my breaths, I found it impossible. Every time I tried, my breath rate changed; it slowed down, even when I tried not to. Just noticing breathing changed my breath rate, so I had to have someone count my breaths for me. I asked a friend to count how many times I breathed in a thirty-second interval without my knowing he was doing it. I asked him to do it a few times and write the numbers down while we were hanging out that day, so I could get an average. Twelve breaths per minute was my average. Fairly good but still not what would be considered an optimal healthy breath.

In the purposeful pursuit of a healthier, slower breath, I've engaged in a lot of breath work where I simply become aware of breathing and slow it down until my mind is needed for the next task. My qigong training taught me that a slower breath usually means longer life. One of my qigong teachers put it to me like this: rats breathe about nine-ty-seven breaths per minute (bpm) and live on average one and a half years. Dogs breathe about twenty-seven bpm but pant as fast as two hundred bpm and live around fifteen years. Americans breathe around fifteen bpm and live around seventy-two years. Giant tortoises breathe one to three bpm and live well over a hundred years. In fact, some tor-toises are known to exceed 140 years, and the legendary white tortoise can live up to three hundred years! Therefore, in Chinese medicine the turtle is revered as a symbol of longevity. There are examples in nature where the breaths per minute and life expectancy don't harmonize in this way, but medical research agrees with the ancient Taoists: for hu-mans, breathe slower to live longer and healthier.

Where a slower breath is healthier and age defying, the opposite is also true. A shorter breath shortens life and creates dis-ease. Many well-known medical institutes have conducted research on the correlation between breathing and health. This research is now plentiful and easy to find. A shorter breath has been linked to hypertension, rheumatoid arthritis, ulcers, asthma, chronic pain, seizures, colitis, irritable bowel syndrome, hyperthyroidism, panic disorder, depression, and a host of mental health disorders including sustained anxiety. Wow! That's a lot of problems from simply not taking a full breath. The panic disorder result brings me back to my own water fear, where I started all of this.

Ever seen someone have a panic attack? Ever had one yourself? Thankfully, I've only had one. The feeling of my breath being complete-ly out of my control made the panic set in much more than the mental anxiety that started the attack in the first place. My fearful thoughts and emotions reached a point where my breathing became involved in what my mind was thinking; my body synchronized up with my mind and chi. My breath became very rapid and extremely shallow, as though I wasn't actually bringing in air at all even though the respiratory pro-cess seemed to be working. The fear that my brain was losing oxygen because of my short, shallow breath caused a more primal fear, or what I'd call actual panic, than the mental stress that started it all off. The panic of mindbody caused the fight-or-flight response to kick into high gear, and the associated rise in adrenaline and cortisol only compounded the intense, overwhelming, all-consuming experience of panic.

The chemical rush was overwhelming on top of the original anxiety. For the first time in my life, I felt like I might pass out. Then I focused in on my breathing: slow, deep breaths. With a little time, the primal fight-or-flight response switched off. With a little more time spent calming my breath, the relaxation response kicked in to gear. More chemical rush; this time it was serotonin calming everything down. The slow, deep breath helped to restore a calmer, more stable frame of mind. The panic and anxiety went away. The residual chemical soup inside me left me utterly exhausted. The thoughts in my head had caused my body to overload.

Out off shore, sitting on my surfboard, drifting, relaxing, breathing slow, I had time to process all this in between the gentle, rolling Florida waves. When I used the meditative breath of a monk (calm, slow, and deep; in and out the nose), I achieved a calmer, more meditative state of mind; quite useful when fighting my fear. When I was focused on the fear, the breath increased and became faster. Calm the breath, calm the fear, face the wave, don't hesitate, paddle, flow, let go. Utilizing the breath, we can control our own chemistry to a great degree. Those almost mythical yogis and ancient qigong masters were right all along, and science is finally starting to catch up and prove it in laboratories across the globe. The ancient Taoist and the mindful surfer have found the same experimental results with the only lab expense being a surfboard.

Breathing, as I was to learn in my surfing/chi training, can also be used to fortify the mind and increase mental focus. There's a qigong breathing technique called warrior breathing that is neither the panicked breath nor the meditative breath, but shares aspects of both. The warrior's breath is full but not slow, deep but not low in the lungs. The warrior's breath is a full breath, in and out the nose, that expands the rib cage, lifting the sternum to the sky. It is not quiet. The inhale is loud and forceful, like trying to breathe in all the oxygen in the room as fast as you can. It's a loud, powerful inhale that's under control. The exhale through the nose is more relaxed, as though the air just falls out of the chest with no effort. The warrior's effort comes when bringing power and energy into the inhale, like a warrior building his internal fire before entering battle. But we can breathe with the fire of desire for a long and healthy life, for a sharp brain and capable body instead of breathing for battle.

When I do this type of breathing, any mental fog I may have had is lifted. I am sharp, aware, energized, oxygenated, and ready to go. Sometimes I use this warrior's breathing in the morning to wake me up, or midday when I need an energy boost, or to clear thoughts or emotions before other engagements. Occasionally I'll use warrior's breathing after a couple of hours of slow-moving tai chi practice just so I don't get too relaxed for the practical needs of the day. The warrior's breath is what I naturally go to when paddling hard and fast to catch a wave. The warrior's breath opens and sharpens my mind with a powerful, energetic boost of oxygen that doesn't cause a crash once it wears off, like sugar or caffeine. It's nature's version of 5-hour Energy: the Breath of Life.

Sitting on my board, waiting for a wave, I had an unexpected flashback. I recalled that years ago I had used breathing to stop smoking cigarettes. That was before I started learning about the breath work of qigong. I grew up with a mom who chain-smoked inside the house, so it's entirely likely I began life addicted to secondhand smoke. I myself started smoking too young, around thirteen, before my body had fully developed, probably because I was addicted to it from infancy. While my mom had the fortitude to quit smoking while she was pregnant, as soon as I popped out, I have no doubt she lit up another menthol cigarette that very birth day. At one point I smoked around half a pack of cigarettes a day. That's about ten cigarettes per day, which is a lot for anyone let alone my still-developing lungs.

Like many other smokers, years into the habit I tried to quit and found it near impossible. I'd stop for a few days or weeks, then pick it right back up again. Throughout this ongoing process, which took place repeatedly for years, the inability to quit left me with low self-esteem: I couldn't even control this voluntary activity of smoking. I felt lame and un-empowered about myself and my life.

One day, during a smoke break at work, I had a bit of a revelation. It suddenly dawned on me that the only time I was taking deep breaths throughout my twelve-hour shifts was when I stepped outside to smoke. It wasn't the tobacco I was craving but the big breath I took with it. Having finally had enough of this filthy habit and armed with this new insight, I decided that whenever I craved a cigarette, I would make myself breathe hard.

At this point I had been doing tai chi for a while, but I had never heard of breath-work training or qigong. I tried to replace the craving for the big tobacco drag with huge, clean breaths of fresh air. It was near impossible for me to do this. For one, I felt silly breathing like that, and when I tried it on breaks at work, my coworkers thought I'd lost it. To make this work I had to DO something that made me take big breaths, like run or do push-ups or jumping jacks when I had the craving. This technique finally worked. Any time I craved a cigarette, I did an exercise really fast that would make me breathe hard right away. Once I had done this for a week or so, I dropped the exercise part because it was inconvenient. Soon I got the hang of taking the big breaths without the exercise, and I was able to simply breathe deeper without the push-up or the cigarette. I no longer had the craving for tobacco; I craved deep breathing instead. I had used breathing to break my lifelong smoking habit.

Breathing can create or destroy health within the body, influence state of mind, and enhance mental focus. So why aren't medical experts

---

---

extolling the benefits of breath work? There are a few medical professionals out there who promote breathing to help heal the body, even some of notoriety like Dr. Oz, who promotes qigong and tai chi. But for the most part, your doctor, like Dr. D, simply won't spend much valuable time helping you understand breathing or practice breathing exercises because there's no kickback pay in that like there is with promoting pharmaceuticals.

Let's be serious about this. It would be difficult for anyone to get rich promoting breathing because everyone already has the physical tools needed. There's nothing to sell. The only thing that one might sell is technique and information, both of which are now readily available on the Internet. To me, that's part of the beauty of this natural medicine: it's free for the taking. We already have the built-in tools to alter our brain chemistry and body health by slightly changing the way we breathe or just becoming aware that we are breathing. We must consciously choose how and when to use the tools we were born with. Every one of us is endowed with the powerful and healing breath of life. So take a moment to notice: Are you breathing?

All can see beauty as beauty only because there is ugliness.
All can know good as good only because there is evil.
Therefore, having and not having arise together.
Difficult and easy complement each other.
High and low rest on one another.
—Lao Tzu, Tao Te Ching

As a forty-three-year-old new surfer, I was super slowly (just like tai chi) beginning to see a glimpse of how surfing is traveling the Tao. I had to work hard to achieve something fluid and soft. My arms were getting stronger from all the paddling, which I hadn't before realized was such a huge part of surfing. In fact, now that I can surf a little bit, I understand that paddling well is a precursor to standing and riding the wave. If you can't paddle out through head-on whitewash, paddle into an appropriate position, and paddle strongly to catch the wave, you probably won't need to try to stand. In fact, I think it was the second day of truly trying to paddle myself into a wave to catch its energy and "ride" it that, later in the afternoon, I could not even raise my arms from my sides, they were so exhausted. It left me feeling weak, humble, and infantile. So glad I didn't have to work that day, as it would have been impossible!

The same is true in tai chi: effortless effort does not come easily. Effortless effort is one of the defining principles of tai chi. This is to use one's will, instead of force or strength, when moving the body or chi; walking the path with conscious intention instead of wandering feet. To not only make it look easy when we slowly stand on one leg and unfurl a hip-high tai chi kick, but to feel that it is easy and effortless is quite difficult to accomplish. When learning my first tai chi form, I thought I had finally gotten it when I had memorized all the Yang short form movements. Little did I realize I had only learned the dance steps and not yet learned the dance. That came only after years of practice. Some pick it up quicker than I did. I admit I am a slow learner. Therefore, tai chi is perfect for me: slow, not rushed in any way. It's also why it took me forty years to pick up a surfboard in earnest.

I have never been in a rush to get anywhere. Where is there to go? This journey ends the same for us all. As the American poet Jim Morrison put it so succinctly, "No one here gets out alive." Since I was so slow to start surfing and tai chi, not beginning either until I was an adult, I brought more introspection to the learning process of both than if I had started at a younger age. Surfing is both difficult and easy. You must paddle strongly but efficiently to get out past the break; then you get to rest a bit, sit, study the waves, and prepare to surf. It's like interval training in that respect. And in the beginning, it doesn't look beautiful. For many, just trying to stay lying on the surfboard while paddling out can be extremely challenging and comical to watch.

New surfers will typically spread out wide on the board in a futile effort to stay balanced in this unfamiliar position. The grom's position typically looks something like a starfish that doesn't know how to float. On top of this unflattering spread-eagle position, the grom usually doesn't plunge her arms deep enough into the water when paddling and

thus throws up streams and sprays of water in an effort that is not effortless, not beautiful, and not propelling her forward very much. Yet if
the grom makes it through the substantial learning curve, nothing can
compare to the beauty of a surfer riding a wave well. This is one of the
reasons it's so appealing: it's simply beautiful to behold the effortless
communion of human and wave by an experienced, skilled surfer. Even
those who don't surf are mesmerized by the human-wave spectacle that
takes place; the effortless effort of a free cosmic energy ride is often
enough to take one's breath away.

We've seen how an unhealthy breath is dis-ease ridden. But what
exactly can all this breath work really do for us, especially if we live in
Oklahoma and don't need to control our fear when going out surfing?
The research is staggering, and there's more of that research coming
out. Healthy breathing creates health. Here are just some of the ways:
Better breathing creates better blood circulation and microcirculation
that feeds the mindbody better than running, where most of the oxygen goes into the straining leg muscles. This increased circulation is
aided by increased oxygen levels when using more lung capacity in a
full breath. Increased microcirculation means better organ function,
better digestive function, better joint and muscle function, and better
brain function. Better brain function equates to better cognitive ability and problem-solving, improved memory, improved motor control,
better stress-coping abilities, more brain plasticity, improved mood,
decreased blood pressure, and an overall sense of well-being. Wow!
That's a lot of benefits from just taking a deeper, slower breath. With
breath work, there are no bad side effects, no costly pills, and no inconvenient checkups.

While beneficial, there's no need to learn any of the complex
breath-work practices provided by various qigong and yoga exercises. If
someone is health compromised or really trying to expand themselves,
finding a qualified instructor who is well versed in breath work or a
class in hatha yoga or qigong can hasten and assist in the healing process. Feedback from an instructor can make things faster and easier, but

is not necessary to benefit from breath work. Simply becoming aware of breathing creates a fuller, deeper, calmer breath. Tuning our awareness to what we're already doing naturally, just becoming mindful, makes the breath healthier—no special exercise required. So just notice breathing; this is enough to improve it.

The science of the mind-body connection came to the forefront at the turn of the twenty-first century largely through the groundbreaking work of Dr. Candace Pert. Dr. Pert was one smart cookie. She was an internationally recognized expert in pharmacology and brain neuro-chemistry with several books and numerous published studies in the field of neuropeptide research.

In her public lectures and books Dr. Pert explained the results and implications of her lab research done when she left the National Institutes for Health. She proved that on a molecular level the mind and body are the same thing. She found in her research that all peptides (the building materials of the body) residing in other areas of the body are also found in the respiratory center.

The connection between the peptide groups in the lungs and their brothers in the rest of the body is the link between why breath work found in qigong and tai chi heals every system in the mindbody. If we can gently coax our breathing into a healthier state by using mindful breathing techniques, then we can control to a large degree the health of our bodies. Because of the neuropeptides' linking mind and body, Dr. Pert used the term *mindbody* as her research showed that, in body and brain chemistry, the mind generates the body. Her research later went on to prove that, at the chemical level, there is no scientific difference between the mind and the body. Therefore, even in her research, she eventually used the term *mindbody*, as indeed there is no separation between the two.

So, a mindful breath (which doesn't cost anything) can be used to heal the mindbody. Not only do centuries of esoteric, empirical Taoist scientists tell me so, but modern Western scientific research backs this up with hard, quantifiable evidence. The breath alone can be used to heal the mindbody. No wonder Dr. D's nutrition supplement worked in studies: they combined it with something that's improved health for centuries: deep breathing!

Imagine a community in which people took responsibility for their own health and well-being by simply using the tools they always have: the breath they take, the movements they make, and the lifestyle they choose to live. While the surfer has a more exotic and photogenic lifestyle than the tai chi master, the surfer usually goes without formal practice of breath work. Yet the breath health of the surfer is enhanced simply because she is in an overly oxygenated environment by being in the ocean. The ocean helps to create oxygen, so the surfer is naturally breathing more oxygenated air.

While there's usually no formal breath-work training on the part of the surfer, awareness of the breath is never far from mind when engaged in a water environment. Sometimes the surfer learns the hard way to be aware of breathing. Even though the Florida coast where I surf is shallow, the force of the waves is often enough to hold me under water. Even if just for a couple of seconds, I'm simply unable to come up for the breath my lungs so desperately want. Many beachgoers drown in the shallow waters of the mid-coastal Atlantic. In one Memorial Day weekend, it was reported that over a hundred beach rescues were made by our local Brevard County lifeguards, all of which happened in mostly chest-deep water. Four beachgoers drowned during that three-day weekend where the waves were small, only about two feet, but quite powerful. Breathing should not be taken for granted by the surfer, beach bunny, or anyone who breathes, if they want to have a long life.

In the way people learn surfing now, the grom slowly starts to integrate diverse ways of breathing depending on what he's doing in the water. Big, full breaths and underwater breath-holding happen automatically when a wave comes at you head-on. Unique styles of rhythmic breathing for the initial paddle-out evolve in the surfer all on their own, just as they evolve for a runner or cyclist, without much awareness at first. There's also the explosive and quick warrior style of breathing unconsciously employed to paddle into and catch a wave. I've seen many surfers do this warrior's breathing naturally without being taught how to breathe in this way that draws in more energy. The surfer just naturally develops a method of breathing that fits with the aspect of what he's doing in the water. But I wonder if way back in the roots of Hawaiian surfing, breath work may have been a conscious and purposeful part of surfing and/or water training.

The most powerful of Hawaiian healers are called the Kahuna Ha, the Masters of the Breath. You've heard of the Big Kahuna. These sacred breath masters use deep-breathing techniques along with spirit-filled dance, hula, and immersion in nature to absorb energy and enhance their own *ha*, or sacred healing breath, for the purpose of healing their community. The very word *aloha* means "meeting of breath" (*alo* = meeting face to face, *ha* = breath of life). *Aloha* is used as a respectful greeting and carries the connotation of love. *Aloha*, Hawaii, breathing, and surfing all go hand in hand it seems. What's not to love about that?

Unfortunately, a lot of us more Western-minded folks don't realize the importance of breathing until it might be too late. When I started teaching qigong, I would occasionally introduce myself as someone who teaches breathing techniques. I quickly learned not to use this wording, as I would often be met with cynical remarks, like, "Pay you to teach me to breathe? Ha! I did that all on my own right from birth." It's usually not until people lose the ability to breathe that they become aware of its importance.

Ted was the perfect example of this. When Ted first came to my outdoor tai chi class, he followed his walker slowly up the path to our shady picnic table and then sat down to rest after his short walk from the parking lot. He had been out of the intensive care unit for two weeks, and both his doctor and his daughter had been encouraging him to take up tai chi for his health. At the time, Ted was seventy-six and had lived a life of fast food, alcohol, and drugs. He himself told me he had been a lifelong, "nasty son of a bitch." While having breakfast at a local restaurant, Ted suddenly turned blue and was taken by ambulance to the hospital. His blood oxygen levels were at 32 percent; normal is 97 percent or higher.

After three days in the intensive care unit and few more in a standard respiratory care room, he could go home. The first day he came to class he was leaning heavily on the walker the whole time. He could only stand about fifteen of the sixty-minute class before he had to sit down at the picnic table, still leaning on the walker for support as he sat. He panted the whole time. He told me he had been diagnosed with COPD (chronic obstructive pulmonary disease), a progressive disorder. By the third time Ted came to class, he no longer had the walker but had to sit down intermittently throughout the session. Within two weeks he was able to stand through more than half the class. After class he told me in private that tai chi was changing his health and his perspective on life. He was realizing how he had never really breathed before coming to our sessions. He practiced diligently on his own every day and continued to bring his cynical humor to all of our outdoor park sessions for a year.

His balance and outlook both continued to improve. At his annual checkup following his ICU incident, his doctor gave him an astounding diagnosis. Ted had worked so diligently to improve his health, he had reversed his COPD! His doctor, who practiced tai chi himself, said he was impressed Ted had chosen to heal himself from this disease that is considered by mainstream medicine to be "irreversible." Along his conscious journey, Ted confided in me that he was now seeing the toxic relationships he had spent years building up all around him, which he had never been aware of before. Breathing and moving more consciously were changing this cynical, hard-hitting, overweight salesman's entire perspective of life, healing him on every level from years of self-abuse. Unfortunately, Ted had to lose his ability to breathe before he would even consider trying to improve it.

The breath master and surfer both learn to integrate breathing techniques into their respective arts and lives. The breath master does it with conscious awareness; the surfer does it without even realizing it—truly just going where the flow takes her. The surfer slowly learns that the initial paddle-out from the beach into the lineup requires a slower-paced, full, rhythmic breath with intermittent BIG breaths and holds while going beneath the oncoming surge of the whitewash. Once the inside-breaking-wave zone has been passed, the paddler then gets to sit on the surfboard, inspecting the incoming waves, and may lose sight of the fact that the breath is naturally returning to a calmer state. Here the surfer is typically preoccupied with observing nature: studying the size, interval, and shape of the incoming waves; noticing the directions of currents and crosscurrents in the water; scanning for ocean wildlife—all the while the breath is naturally calming down from the initial paddle-out.

At some point, the surfer makes the mental commitment to ride a specific incoming wave. Here she turns the board toward the shore, starts the fast, powerful paddle strokes required to catch the wave, and unknowingly switches to a warrior's type of breathing—fast but full connected breaths to pull in as much oxygen and power as possible in order to match the speed of the wave—which must be done in order to catch it, to synch up with its cosmic energy. It is here that any number of events may ensue that determine how the surfer breathes while out in the ocean environment. Depending on what happens with the wave once synchronized with it, the surfer may hold the breath, accelerate the breath more, return it to a rhythmic paddle-back-out rate, or even just turn out of the wave and return immediately to a relaxed, "normal" breath. No matter which it is, the surfer is constantly varying the breath between full/hold, fast/slow, calm/intense. Truly, this is breath work whether the surfer is aware of it or not.

It's my experience that since those who are in the ocean a lot are naturally doing breath work, they are rewarded with better overall health and well-being. Surfers take much bigger breaths and hold them for longer than those who don't get in the water, thereby absorbing more oxygen and chi energy. That big ocean-air breath also holds salt particles, which we know is a natural detoxifier and healer. So, the surfer's lungs are continually detoxifying and expanding and absorbing higher concentrations of healing oxygen. This has tremendous effects on the health and well-being of the practitioner/surfer. This is the breath of life, and when exercised, is a most profound and powerful tool.

So, the surfer is actively engaged in breath work even though he might not be conscious of it. Breath work is a major aspect of qigong, which can be translated to mean breath work: *qi/chi* = breath or energy, *gong* = work. The surfer's regular practice of breath work is creating better overall health of not only body but mind and emotion as well. This is one part of why I propose that to surf mindfully is to become a Taoist, one who utilizes the tools of nature to live in better harmony and balance.

Nothing is more soft and yielding than water.
Yet for attacking the strong and solid, nothing is better;
The weak can overcome the strong;
The supple can overcome the stiff.
Everyone knows this,
Yet no one puts it into practice.
The truth often sounds paradoxical.
—Lao Tzu, Tao Te Ching

The idea of balance and harmony between opposites is inherent in the taiji symbol representing yin and yang. The Western mind often interprets this as opposites, the black and white opposing each other. The Taoist mind and the scientist see the balance of the polarity needed for the fire of existence. Without polarity, there is no movement of energy. It is the positive and the negative of the battery that make the battery work. It simply must have both, or it won't work. The simplicity and truth of this had been sung to me a good portion of my life, but it wasn't until it was said in a certain way that it finally struck a chord in me. Yet it took the wisdom of a stranger in my future to show me just how deep the taiji symbol goes.

Living so close to the ocean now in Satellite Beach made it much easier to surf. It was so convenient to just walk to the beach when I had free time and assess the conditions to decide if I wanted to surf or not. Mersea had taught me about the online, live beach cameras that showed the conditions in many surf spots. There was even a camera on the beach two blocks from my house. Those camera websites also had online surf forecasts. It didn't take long to learn that the forecasts were often wrong or off a day or two. A live peek at the conditions is still the best way to determine if you want to go out or not.

I was paddling out to surf more often, sometimes a few times a day when I could, and my skills were improving. After three-plus years of surfing, I was no longer considered a grom, but I sure felt like one every single time I went out. I still had to work at controlling my fear. I need-ed the mental safety net of having other people nearby on the beach to paddle out, but now I'd go out as the sole surfer in the water. This was an enormous step despite having to consciously breathe and relax myself the entire session. Whenever another surfer paddled out, even a few blocks away, I was grateful for and relieved a little by the company. I wouldn't yet challenge myself with bigger than chest-high waves, even if Mersea went out, encouraging me to come along. And other surfers in the lineup near me often got waves that were set up perfectly for me just because I was too passive to try to out-paddle someone, and I let them have it instead of even trying. I had progressed in skill but had a long way to go when it came to courage.

My new teacher, Grand Master Cook, helped change that. The qi-gong exercise known as *yi jin ching* was teaching me to center myself in my own strength. It was a more physically strengthening practice than I was used to in qigong. Up to this point in my life, I was noticeably qui-et, demure, and passive; extremely yin in my interactions with others. I had never really asserted myself in my relationships with coworkers, family, friends, or partners. I had always gone along with what others wanted, even if I might not like it, just because it was easier for me to do than to extend myself. The philosophy "It's better to be seen than heard" comes to mind.

As I practiced *yi jin ching* under Grand Master Cook's watchful eye, I could feel myself becoming more balanced in every way. My body became stronger and more symmetrical; my life-force chi energy was at an all-time high (here, well into my forties); my ambitions and mind were clearer and more focused. My self-confidence grew. Up to now, even though I might have been surfing next to a bunch of less experienced people, I always let others have the wave, which they frequently did not catch, and that perfect wave would roll into shore unridden, an excellent opportunity passing me by.

Even if a wave was coming in that was perfect for me, coming right to me with me sitting in the perfect takeoff spot, I would not try to take it if another person was trying to catch it. But with my confidence building through *yi jin ching* practice, I started to paddle for more waves. I was beginning to let go of that passive child I had always been comfortable being and assert myself more. I was now willing to try to out-paddle the guy beside me to see who got the privilege of riding the wave.

To you this might not seem important, so let me detail just a little of what I was going through. I was a scared-out-of-my-mind, "older," unconfident woman usually surfing among much younger, stronger, aggressive males. It was not always friendly. I was frequently laughed at by groups of pubescent boys floating nearby, striving to prove their manliness by insulting the lone "old woman." I was called granny on several occasions and told to go home and knit a sweater. I never got this treatment from solo surfers; only when they were a pack. On top of this, I did not yet have my water fear contained. I did not move as quickly or easily as these local boys who had been surfing since age five with their bros. My very exposed body was not as agile as theirs were, and I was quite self-conscious of the fact that I could not hide behind clothes out here. I was exposed with bare skin, and what wasn't bare was covered in skin-tight wet clothes, so I was very aware of how I must look to these boys: old and slow. It was not always hostile in the lineup, but for passive me, it was often intimidating. Up until this point in my life, I had always given way.

Now, *yi jin ching* was building my strength, confidence, and assertiveness. I started taking more waves, and because of that, my skill and confidence grew more. Here, at forty-plus years old, I was starting to learn how to claim my place in the world and not let others take what was clearly mine. I started to become more balanced. During these years of learning balance through surfing and tai chi training, as my confidence grew, I was also learning to let go more, to relax more, to not let things get to me.

This lesson tested me in a very real, tangible financial way: I lost my steady, reliable source of income. Dr. D sold the small business I had been working at for five years, and I was let go. I had been in a wonderful position working just three days a week, able to set my own schedule, and still able to pay all my bills. This fantastic job that I loved had allowed me plenty of time to surf and perfect my tai chi and qigong lessons.

It's said in various spiritual traditions to beware of the person seeking mastery of self, for her path will be fraught with obstacles and hardships to test her and her resolve. I felt like this job loss was one of those life-changing tests. In my midforties now, I had spent my whole life free from financial worries. I had never had an excess of money, but I had always had a little savings and a small but steady paycheck to make me feel financially secure. I had just lost that sense of security.

My morning and night reading of the heady *Tao Te Ching*, the surf, the beach, the sun, the rolling water, the floating and drifting in the sea, deep breathing and meditation, the rhythmic currents of the ocean within me and around me, combined with the intense tai chi and qigong, had put me in a position to just let go and drift mindfully into the unknown. I did not get another job. Instead, I started teaching donation-based tai chi and qigong classes outdoors in the local parks, expanding classes I had started at Dr. D's. I relied on my tiny savings, frugal living (even in the sultry Florida summer I did not run my air conditioning), and miniscule tai chi income to float me for a while, with no other career or financial plan. I consciously let go of who I had been.

When I left the corporate work world, which controls most aspects of life in America, I had to come to grips with the fact that I was giving up a regular paycheck so I could teach tai chi, which is not, unfortunately, in high demand. This was very scary at first. To not have any guarantee of income is a daunting prospect. Yet I walked into this emptiness knowing it is only when we become empty that we can be filled. When I am satisfied with what I have, I never want for more.

Just like those first baby steps out of my comfort zone and into the ocean, for me it was terrifying. When I realized I was going to be poor but still able to pay my few bills, I let go and relaxed some more. My surfing improved as well as my tai chi forms. My shifu noticed the change, saying I was flowing better and moving with more confidence from my center. Tai chi was becoming a literal representation of my daily life; the opposite was also true. I was starting to take notice and become more aware. My mind was letting go of its tight grip on who I had been, and I was starting to see more of what was right in front of me all the time: the Tao is the Way.

Being dirt poor wasn't so bad. I'd been here before. I knew how to do it gracefully without suffering. After teaching a couple of years, my classes began to grow and my income increased a little, but it still dropped off entirely in the summer months when all the older, retired snowbirds went back to their northern states for a cooler summer than what we sweated through here in central Florida. That being so, I had to produce creative ways to make money that wouldn't put me locked back in a non-flowing nine-to-five regimented, unnatural schedule.

As a Taoist surfer, I needed to produce diverse ways to make money so that I had enough open time to surf when the conditions were good. Before I lost my comfortable job, a coworker went to South America on a trip using a new and, at the time, unknown website called Airbnb.

I remembered it and checked it out now that I needed more income. I saw the current wave of energy and decided to take it for myself. Seems I had the perfect place to rent out a room to tourists: walking distance to a beach in central Florida. I wound up hosting tourists from all over the world and got exposed to a new way to travel and many ways to live.

To my surprise, I never had a guest who was a surfer despite being so close to well-known surf spots. But I did get a few visitors to fall in love with surfing before they left. This makes me happy, as I feel I've "paid forward" the surf life that Mersea so patiently introduced me to. It felt very full circle to turn my guests on to surfing. I loaned them boards from my now-ample collection and gave them simple lessons and some company on their very first paddle-outs, just as Mersea had done for me. It felt as though, by the simple act of sharing surfing with others, I was helping the entire world breathe a little easier. That's when I met another guide in my Taoist studies, someone who knew absolutely nothing about tai chi.

I had been renting out my small spare bedroom to tourists for a year when one of my most profound teachers, the Swede, came to rest for a while by the sea. He was a tall, refined Swedish engineer in his seventies on a recuperative holiday for a month. He was here alone and was to meet up with his daughter in New York after he spent a month at my place beside the ocean so he could restore his cancer-ravaged body. He was utterly fastidious with his diet, eating only organic and nutrient-dense food. At his urging, I accompanied him to a small, local organic restaurant for lunch. As we settled into a corner table, he asked me a puzzling question: "What is this tai chi you do?"

He had been staying with me for just three days at this point, and I was caught off guard a little by his simple but complicated question. I wasn't sure how to respond. No one had put it to me quite this way before. Being an instructor for a few years now, it was easy to answer the usual questions, like, "How does this help my health?" "Why do you have to move so slowly?" and "Will this help my balance?" I could quote Harvard medical research on the numerous mindbody benefits of tai chi. I could get a Western mind to comprehend the necessity of balancing fast life with slow life. I had even inspired a successful seventy-five-year-old self-made millionaire to practice cultivating chi every day. But I wasn't immediately sure how to answer this question from my savvy, world-traveling guest.

Luckily, our waitress came and I caught a moment to collect and summarize my thoughts on the question before I had to answer this logically minded engineer who'd been working to overcome cancer for several years. "Well," I started out, "tai chi is an ancient Chinese form of moving meditation that combines breathing exercises, visualizations, and specific, precise movements as a form of preventative health care." I thought I had summarized well enough to satisfy this sophisticated, practical mind.

"So, it's exercise and movement of some sort?"

"You could say that," I responded. "It's also learning stillness in motion, and there are meditations where there are no external movements at all, only internal. This is usually referred to as *qigong* (energy work), or more specifically *nei gong* (internal work)."

"Stillness in motion," he replied slowly, leaning into the table toward me. "This I think I'm beginning to understand."

He continued, "In my quest to heal from cancer and the treatment of the cancer, I explored many avenues of healing. I worked with physiotherapists, nutritionists, MDs of course, and I also started going to workshops at a local Swedish shop that put on yoga and pranic healing and drumming and shamans and all that sort of thing. I was attending a meditation, and the presenter proposed that we must be still to heal, but that in our stillness we should not be empty but focused on being healed. Not focusing on getting healed, not becoming healed, but being healed. And that in simply *being* we would find healing, whether that healing be from physical, emotional, or psychic damage." Our meals arrived, and the conversation turned to nutrition and the need for organics, especially when healing a dis-eased body.

After we had leisurely enjoyed lunch, he leaned back in his chair, obviously savoring the moment, smiled widely, and changed back to our former topic: "So from the meditation talks at the little shop, I slowly started to realize that this meditation teacher was talking about balancing our *doing* with our *being*. I came to understand that sometimes it is the doing and the overdoing that can make us sick and that we need to simply be to create balance in our bio-organisms. I thought about this for some time and started to practice beingness every chance I got, and I discovered that this teacher was right.

"When I took the time to stop running around to heal myself, like the madman clinging to life that I was, running from this doctor to that, to the nutritionist, to the movement therapist, to the lab, to the acupuncturist— When I stopped some of that and ended all the rushing around, and I was just *being* grateful for the health I had, I started to feel better. After a while I came to realize I needed to fully embrace a Frank Sinatra lifestyle." He had a sly but meaningful grin on his splotchy face.

"What do you mean by 'Frank Sinatra lifestyle'?" I asked.

"Well, what's one of the most famous Frank Sinatra songs? What quickly comes to mind when you think of him?"

While I am American and should be familiar with our best-known classic crooner, I am quite a bit younger than my engineer guest, and I couldn't quickly think of any songs by Old Blue Eyes. "I don't know. Uh . . . *do be do be do*," I crudely crooned and then laughed, not even sure if it was one of Frank's tunes.

"Exactly," he beamed and leaned into the table, locking eyes with me. He said very slowly, "*Do be do be do*. We must balance our *doing* with our *being*. Too much being, and we can become lazy; too much doing, and we become stressed and sick. So, I think Frank Sinatra must have been a tai chi master, don't you?" He leaned back and stretched out in his chair as he smiled keenly at me with a gleam in his eyes

My mouth must have been hanging open. My mind was reeling at how simply he had summed up "What is this tai chi?" by quoting a pop-culture icon. I was astounded, inspired, and as giddy with hearing it as the Swede was with telling it. We both simply smiled for a moment until the waitress collected our empty plates. "You know," I said, "maybe Frank Sinatra *was* a tai chi master." We both laughed at the knowing, secret collusion of blindingly obvious knowledge hidden in plain sight. The Tao is the Way.

To be honest, I was embarrassed that I hadn't really given the yin-yang symbol a lot of thought until the Swede brought up the "*do be do be do*." Do/be = yang/yin.

You'd think that, as a tai chi teacher, I would have thought a little more about the black-and-white symbol that represents tai chi and the philosophy of the Tao. I knew it represented the yin and the yang, and that there's a little of yin in yang and vice versa, represented by the two dots near the middle of the circle. I knew it was called a taiji, not "a yin-yang," as most people call it, meaning it was a visual representation of all there is, the grand ultimate, the Tao. I knew that the black yin part represents stillness, or *beingness*. And the white yang part was the *doingness* of activity.

As a tai chi player, I knew that the "yin foot" is the empty, unweighted foot and the "yang foot" is the foot that is full and has our weight. As our weight is often distributed between our feet in various proportions of balance, this is represented in the taiji by the two dots. But I had never really thought about what the symbol was or meant. I was humbled by the Swede's simple and accurate perception of this ancient symbol and the physical act of tai chi. I was utterly compelled to explore this further.

That which shrinks must first expand.
That which fails must first be strong.
That which is cast down must first be raised.
Before receiving, there must be giving.
This is called perception of the nature of things.
The soft and weak overcome the hard and strong.
—Lao Tzu, Tao Te Ching

After my enlightening lunch with the Swede, I decided to start studying the taiji symbol in earnest. Thousands of books have been written on the subject, so it can feel a little overwhelming and hard to know where to start. To my amazement, the day after our lunch, my email inbox held an invitation to a free webinar on yin and yang hosted by an acupuncturist. Looked like I was being shown where to start; just go with the flow.

In the taiji symbol, black is yin and white is yang. The symbol can be viewed in terms of a twenty-four-hour day. A day is one thing that's divided into two: night and day. An entire day moves through both night and daytime, so both parts are necessary for the whole. Since blackness happens at night, yin can be associated with nighttime and the energies of that time of day. White therefore represents the daytime and the energies associated with that time. To me, this was blatantly the two sides of Frank Sinatra's coin: we *do* in the day and we simply *be* in the night. I like that it didn't stop there with Frank. It repeats again and again and again: *do be do be do*. Just like day and night. Just because one is over doesn't mean it won't come back around. Traditionally, we understand that the taiji symbol is turning, spinning around its center, just like day and night: cycling on and on and on. One always changing into the other, rarely all yin or all yang, but morphing back and forth between the two.

In the night, energies are naturally slower, more even and still, when we are sleeping. Most creatures of the natural world rest in the night, but not all; just as some are more active in the day, but not all. The moon, mostly visible at night, is considered yin, while the sun is considered yang. This makes sense within the balance of activity and inactivity. The moon in the yin night is a lifeless, inactive, passive rock with nothing taking place on it. The sun, where millions of hydrogen explosions take place continually, is a hotbed of yang activity. And this from the webinar is curious: What creature is often associated with the sun? The lion. When active, not much of anything can withstand the sheer yang power of a hunting lion. The yin side of the lion is that they are known to sleep for as much as fourteen hours a day. This makes the lion one of the most yin of yang beasts!

This night-and-day comparison of the taiji also holds true within the idea that one becomes the other. Within the symbol, black tapers off into white and vice versa, allowing its companion to become fully itself. Night gradually becomes day, and day gradually becomes night. Night does not become day all at once. It's a gradual shift until day is completely day with no moon or stars to be seen. So, it's not a straight-line, linear shift. This is seen in the center curve of the taiji: there is not a straight line between yin and yang, but a curving center line that continues turning when viewed with the symbol spinning. This is the ever-changing, ongoing cycle of *do be do be do* that is the nature of our world. Doing in the day, being in the night. Each needing the other to simply exist; not opposing but supporting each other.

It was challenging, but thinking about surfing in terms of yin and yang helped distract me from the fear, which was weakening its grip on me. Now that I had gotten past the infant-like grom stage, I sometimes forced myself to paddle out where there was no one else in the water so I could work on overcoming the fear on my own, without the support of others. I often just sat out past the breaking waves thinking and digesting what I was learning about yin and yang.

I learned that, in a traditional perspective, water is considered yin and fire is considered yang. Therefore, in antiquity, and sometimes even today, the taiji symbol was not black and white, but blue and red. In terms of surfing and waves, I see the yin as the land (still/be) and the yang as the water (active/do). Both land and water are required for a wave to form. As the energy (or chi) travels through the water toward land it remains subtle, almost imperceptible, over the depths of the open ocean. It's not until that energy gets close to or passes over higher land on the bottom that the surface of the ocean jacks up and creates a wave.

The seeming opposites of land and water are both required to create a wave: two parts forming one whole. As anyone who's spent time with the waters of the earth knows, the influence of the moon on tides and waves is quite profound. When the moon is full, the high tide is higher than usual and so are the waves. When the moon is dark, the low tides are lower than usual and so are the waves. Yet it is the energy emanating from the active, yang sun passing through the atmosphere creating heat and wind that stirs the waters of the oceans. So, it is the combined power of these seeming opposites of sun and moon that determines the existence and the intensity of the wave.

And what of the wave itself? Is it not an ever-changing flow of energy that never ceases in its cycle? Yes, to the dismay of surfers all over the world, the ocean does sometimes go completely flat with nothing but mirror images of the sky and clouds for amusement. But this too fades, and the waves eventually return. As I sat alone in the ocean, resting on my surfboard between waves, I thought of the energy of the cosmos combining with Earth's energy to create the unique, one-time-only opportunity to ride the galactic chi as it manifests in rideable waves near the shoreline.

Every wave is different, yet all have the same basic spiraling Fibonacci configuration that propels my surfboard forward on the crest of galactic chi. For the wave to break, it must curve, just like the center curve of the taiji. Even though the momentum of the galactic energy is pushing forward toward the shore, when it meets the uprising land obstacle, a small bit of the energy retreats, moving away from the shore and creating the trough of the wave. It is this retreat that creates the trough out of which the crest of the breaking wave also forms. While the bottom energy of the wave retreats, the forward momentum of the uprising water lifts that retreating energy and sucks it over, creating a powerful, spiraling, breaking wave. The yin retreating water generates the yang forward-breaking wave. The opposite is also true: if not for the forward-moving yang wave, the yin trough would never form. *Do be do be do.*

As large fish stir beneath the surface of the water near me, I distract myself with reason: therefore, it is only in the yin of the retreating energy that the yang power of that energy can be expressed. Both are necessary for the single wave to exist. To me this is more evidence of the Tao of surfing. When there is balance between yin and yang, harmony is achieved. The Way of nature unfolds in the spiral energy patterns found throughout all of existence, including our very own DNA.

Having now been both a non-surfer and a surfer, I can understand Harvard psychologist Dr. Timothy Leary's arrogant statement that "in the evolution of our species, the surfer has found the ultimate balanced lifestyle." To be a surfer means embracing the ways of nature and learning to work in harmony with galactic chi. The surfer must learn not only to become yang and *do* by actively riding the spiraling wave, but also how to *be* yin and wait patiently for the wave as it rolls in, or when the surf's gone flat, know that eventually it will come back around again.

The galactic wave rider must learn balance in an ever-changing field or ocean of energy. To stand up and then walk on water, even with a surfboard under foot, requires a kinesthetic awareness of one's core, one's center. While aware of the core, the surfer must also be aware of her vertical axis. If she leans too far forward or back, she will fall or leave the power point of the wave's energy. The surfer also understands her relationship to the horizontal axis. She is fully aware of everything going on around her: other people in the water, the direction the wave is going, scanning for underwater rocks, etc. In the view of world-re-nowned author and peacemaker Thich Nat Hanh, to understand one's horizontal axis means to understand our relationship to everything around us. To relate to one's own vertical axis means to have a connection to both the earth beneath us and the heavens above. In tai chi and qigong, we reference our physical vertical axis in our awareness of self and posture; we reference our horizontal axis in the awareness of our relationships within the environment on the horizontal plane.

The dedicated surfer must have a flexible lifestyle so that he's able to drop what he's doing to paddle out when the surf is good, but also be able to accept when there is no surf. Surfers often become entre-preneurs and business owners so they can close the shop with a Gone Surfing sign when the waves are good. When I first got the idea to surf my water fear away, I had an image of being able to paddle out in the ocean and work toward my goal whenever I had the time, since I lived so close to the beach. I very quickly realized that the ocean, not me, is typically in charge of when I go out. This is staggering and perception changing to those of us who've always had a tight control on our schedules.

With every other sport or activity, I could always go whenever I had the time and felt like it. Running? Just go. Biking? Roll when you want to. Golf with Dad? Set up a tee time, which would occasionally get interrupted by rain, but not often. Basketball? Find a hoop; they're easy to find indoors and out. Hiking? Available any time of day; occasionally weather prevails. Usually, I can do whatever I want, when I want. I'm in charge.

Not so with surfing. Just because I have some time and the weather is nice doesn't mean there will be waves to ride. Sometimes the ocean is completely flat, like a lake. During the summer in Florida that flatness can last for months on end: the surfer's summertime blues. Often, the ocean is so rough that even if there are waves, it is impossible to ride them, like trying to catch a current in the slosh of a washing machine. The wind plays a huge part in the conditions, which is why it's usually better to surf in the morning, before the wind kicks up. Wind coming onshore, from behind the wave, can push the wave flatter so it doesn't form into a peak, making it ridiculously hard or impossible to catch. Wind coming offshore can knock the tops off the waves or hold the waves up, creating a barrel- or tube-like effect. Winds coming from the sides are also variable in how they affect the surf. The wind also affects my longboard. Sometimes an offshore wind will lift the long nose of the board, making it difficult to drop down the face of the wave. The wind is holding the board in the air like a kite or sail, so it doesn't want to drop down with the descending energy of the wave. I've lost many waves simply because the wind held the surfboard back from catching the energy.

The tide too makes a substantial difference. There have been times when I missed the only small window of opportunity to surf in a day because I had an appointment during the best tidal conditions. If the tide is high, it can make the shoreline water too deep so that the waves don't really break. High tide can also make exceptionally large surf a little bit smaller and more manageable. Low tide can pull all the energy out of the wave, making it super small and weak. Low tide can also cause the wave to break in very shallow water, which can be quite dangerous in rocky conditions. This, unfortunately, took me a few years to figure out, and I will forever bear the scars of being thrown into rocks during low tide. The same low tide can also pull the energy out of the wave, making it break hollower and more tube-like. It all just depends on the conditions; every day and every wave are different.

Unbelievably, clouds versus a cloudless sky also influence the surf conditions. It's usually easier to see the waves as they roll in when it's cloudy, making it easier to be in an appropriate position to catch the ride. When it's cloudy, the water also looks more haunting, dark, and mysterious, and can sometimes be spooky, as it's more difficult to see deeper into the water beyond the surface. When the sky is clear and the sun is shining, it's easier to see into the water, making it bluer, more inviting, and fun. But when the sun is too bright or at an angle, it can reflect off the water to the degree that it becomes impossible to see the incoming waves; this makes it difficult to catch them simply because of being blinded by the sun.

So many different variables influence the wave conditions that here in Florida it's only occasionally what would be called "good" surf. In fact, I've been told that to surf in Florida is a lesson in patience and perseverance compared to other places in the world where the surf is more consistent. In the early learning stage especially, the conditions are super important. If it's not good and easy, then it's not fun or enjoyable, and hard to keep doing it. To be a surfer in Florida, you must really want to. You must be patient and willing to go out when conditions are not optimal. You must be willing to "eat bitterness," as the Chinese would say.

Personally, I think it's the difficulty of learning to surf in this area that has produced some of the world's top-ranking surfers. Some notable names in surfing have come from along these hundred miles of Florida coastline. Many people around the globe are familiar with the name Kelly Slater, the most dominant athlete in all of sports. Kelly grew up in Cocoa Beach and has now won more world surf titles than any other surfer. At over forty years old he is still in the professional arena, competing against guys in their teens and twenties.

Kelly's brother Stephen Slater is also a world champion in longboard surfing.

There are many other notable surfers who've sprung from central Florida shores, among them one of the most dominant and groundbreaking women in surfing: Lisa Andersen. Being a talented surfer and photogenic made it possible for Lisa Andersen to exponentially grow women's surfing. While other women surfers were talented and capable, few combined the sheer athletic drive and fearlessness of Lisa with wholesome, girl-next-door good looks. Because of this, Lisa was the first woman surfer to ever appear on the cover of the male-dominated surf magazines. This gave rise to women being viewed as legitimate surf athletes instead of beach-bunny arm-candy for their surfing boyfriends. Despite this, it wasn't until 2017 that women were finally allowed to compete in the prestigious big-wave surf event known as the Eddie Aikau Memorial. This world-class event only takes place when the waves tower over twenty feet in Waimea Bay on Oahu's famous North Shore. Very slowly, the yin feminine aspects are beginning to balance out the yang, male-dominated surf world.

While the surf along this stretch of Florida is good enough to get you hooked into the sport, it's not consistent enough to make it easy to surf here. Therefore, a surfer wannabe must work really hard to learn to surf here and to continue surfing here. This gives our local wave-riders a training advantage over those in other parts of the world where the surf might be more consistently better. Here, you must surf in both good and not so good conditions, which is the case for professional surf competitions. You can't schedule a week-long event involving media and thousands of people only to throw it all away if the surf's not so great. Because of this, the local surfers here have a competitive advantage over those who only surf great conditions, and thus some the world's best surfers continue to emerge from our waters.

With all this, it becomes quickly evident to the new surfer that she is not in charge of the surf schedule, the ocean is. This can be very humbling for a Western mind that's always in the driver's seat, directing when and where to go. Yet when immersed in the ways of nature, Nature is in charge. This is a very Taoist sentiment that may feel familiar from many Chinese landscape paintings. In this Taoist style, it is not the human that has dominance on the canvas but nature. The human is present yet small, in the background, sometimes hidden and barely seen. The entire scene is of the mountain, field, lake, river, ocean, or such with the human element appearing as an afterthought.

The Taoist understanding is that while man is in Nature, he cannot dominate it. The new surfer begrudgingly learns he is not always in charge. Nature and the cyclical laws of nature always have the final say, regardless of our ego. This is learning how to let go of what we want so that we may accept things as they are. Letting go of *doing* the human experience and simply *being* the human experience. This is an unbelievably valuable lesson, one that some people rarely let themselves experience. To not be in total control can feel very outside of our comfort zone, yet this is part of the natural cycle of yin and yang.

When we *do*, we feel a form of active power, the yang side of our ego, exerting control. Here, in the depth of activity, we somehow feel we are in control of our lives. *We* are in charge. *We* get things done. In a culture where we *do* in order to reach where society tells us we should be—in charge, in control, on point, always on, always doing, achieving, more, more, more—to simply *be* in a society of *doers* can appear counterproductive and quite unnatural. It is leaving the familiar comfort of always *doing*. And because *being* doesn't produce more of any tangible thing, *being* is seen as undesirable. If you're not producing, Western, yang-centric society judges you as "less than."

When we won't make the time to simply *be* on a regular basis, we become out of balance. We are no longer able to relax at all, often slowly moving into a crisis of life-altering nature, just like me kicking and punching myself right out of work. Our own obsessive *doing* can cause us to slow down and take a break. Usually, when it happens this way, it's not fun. We can work ourselves into a cancerous situation like the

Swede confessed to. We keep engaging in an activity we know is hurting us until one day it hurts us so badly, we're in the hospital. We keep punching and kicking things in rage, and our bodies simply break, so we can't use them and must slow down and evaluate ourselves to correct the issue. We need the *be* part of our human experience. We need to *do be do be do* to find balance in the ultimate Frank Sinatra lifestyle.

In surfing we can find both: we *do* when we paddle and work the wave; we *be* when we sit and wait. In tai chi and qigong, we find both as well: we *do* in our slow, mindful movements; we *be* in our seated and standing mediations: Stand. Relax. Breathe. Eventually, in both surfing and tai chi, we reach a place of balance where we are both *doing* and *being* at the same time. This happens when we reach the state of mindful stillness while still engaged in our activity. It is here that we have finally attained effortless effort, stillness within movement. We can achieve both the *doing* and the *being* at the same time, balancing yang and yin.

Despite the swirling stress of our world, everyone has the ability and opportunity to attain a healthy, balanced, Frank Sinatra lifestyle. It doesn't happen overnight, though. It takes time to become one with the flow, learning to let go even while moving. To move into "the zone," as athletes call it. Here time changes, nothing else exists except experiencing the moment in its fullness, connecting with the energy of the experience, flowing with it in harmony; movements become effortless, quiet takes over, a particular ease and calm settle into the mindbody, and we feel not only at peace but one with the moment, one with existence, one with the field of all that is.

Most people have experienced this at some point in their lives. Certain events trigger this state automatically: a loving wedding, the birth of a child. Here we often exist, if momentarily, in an elevated state, within a state of consciousness that most people reach only rarely. A few people push themselves to experience this state consciously and at will. The tai chi player with enough practice will be able to attain this state of peace and oneness at will. He may not begin learning tai chi with this intention, but with enough practice this ability is attained.

It is the same with surfing. Eventually, by engaging in the activity enough, the surfer will get good enough at the sport to be able to move into a heightened state of awareness, a feeling of oneness with the wave, the energy of the ocean, and all there is in that moment. By continuing to engage this state of "no mind" where awareness is piqued but thoughts end, by being here over and over and over and over, the surfer and the chi practitioner are conditioning the mindbody to remain in a heightened state of consciousness. A state where you don't get mad when someone cuts you off in traffic. You don't have the desire to yell at anyone. You feel peaceful and calm even during times of stress, when your life and the world may be topsy-turvy. You can maintain your center, your calm; you can keep your peace. Some people, of course, are better at it than others, as in all things. Few would be able to remain as fearless as Mersea and paddle without hesitation into a huge school of sharks. But eventually, without even knowing it, the dedicated surfer reshapes his perception of the world, going from seeing what he wants to seeing things as they are and flowing mindfully with them. The ultimate Frank Sinatra lifestyle: *do be do be do.*

It is not wise to rush about.
Let all things come and go effortlessly, without desire.
If too much energy is used, exhaustion follows.
This is not the way of Tao.
Whatever is contrary to Tao does not last long.
—Lao Tzu, Tao Te Ching

Now, at forty-five years old, I started learning how to let go of my tight grip of fear-fueled control. When I went out to surf, I could let my body relax more. Sitting on my board now felt natural as I became more adapted to the water environment that had so terrorized me in the past. I was finally starting to release my fear. In this letting go, I began to feel the energy of the ocean more instead of waiting in anticipation of what I wanted. When I relaxed more on the surfboard, I could feel shifting currents in the water I hadn't felt before, crosscurrents, little swirling eddies. I began to accept what was instead of what I desired. In this, I began to see things as they are, from a more objective, less me-centered perspective.

This letting-go aspect of surfing takes place on another level, one that's very relative to tai chi training and can have profound effects on the practitioner. The fluid grace of the surfer and of the tai chi player both come from letting go of excess muscular tension. Use "effortless effort," as Lao Tzu put it. Most people use more muscular effort in day-to-day activities than they must. It takes extraordinarily little effort to hold one's hands over a keyboard, resting on a desk. Yet most computer workers develop neck and shoulder pain due to tension in these muscles. I still catch myself all the time pulling my shoulders up to my ears when I'm typing at a keyboard. I'm sure I'm not alone in this one simple example.

Using too much muscular effort creates more toxins in the body, makes muscles sore, and uses up precious energy. How many times have you felt tired at the end of the day when you really haven't done enough to warrant low energy? This often happens to us when we use too much muscular effort to simply move through the activities of the day. This uses up our energy just as lifting weights does, leaving us tired even though we might not have done much in the way of physical activity.

Letting go of our excess muscular tension is a key component of tai chi training. Just to take a step with as little effort as possible is quite challenging. Try it sometime. In tai chi training, we learn how to put our foot on the ground with no weight on it at first, using as little muscular effort as possible. It takes somewhere around two hundred different muscles to simply take a step forward. Being aware of all these muscles at the same time and using as little energy as possible to move them in harmony takes a lot of focus and self-awareness. In fact, it takes more focus to let go of muscles than it does to engage them.

The benefits of this effortless effort in movement are numerous. We use less energy to move our bodies; therefore we have more energy. We don't generate as many biotoxins; therefore our immune systems aren't working so hard and we are healthier overall. We relax more, which means we experience less stress, the health benefits of which are enormous. With all these physical benefits to letting go, it's easy to overlook the deeper, more meaningful benefits. When we let go of our excess muscular tension, we allow our own energy to flow better within us. We loosen our grip, or control, a bit and in so doing become aware of the subtle flows of energy within us and in our external environment as well. We let go of what we know in order to learn something more than that.

This is one of the most amazing side effects of tai chi training: to simply let go is freeing. It takes a lot of effort to hold on to something, but no effort to let go of it. Whether holding on to ideas, people, things, or relationships—all require a lot of effort to keep and maintain when we try to control them. When we don't try to direct how they unfold, they become effortless, less rigid, more flowing.

Sitting out past the break zone on my used longboard waiting for waves, I let the ocean hold me. Instead of trying to rigidly control every aspect of the board and keep it still, I simply let go of my grip and moved with the bobbing board. In this small release of control, I began to better understand how the surfboard moved and planed with the currents. I noticed the subtler aspects of the currents and crosscurrents beneath me. Up until now I had used my eyes to tell me which way to paddle so I could catch the most energy from the wave. I saw which direction the wave was going, and I went that way, typically straight at the shoreline.

Now I noticed there were multiple currents going on unseen beneath the surface. I could feel that the energy of an incoming wave was going slightly to the south instead of directly west to the shore. In letting go of my muscular grip on the surfboard, I was able to allow more information to come in. Understanding this slight current difference helped me catch more waves; thus my surfing improved. Letting go sitting on the surfboard was becoming more effortless and natural, making it easier to paddle with the current of the wave, making it easier to catch. The ride itself was flowing better as well. With my muscles relaxing more now, my awareness was growing, my surfing was flowing, and my fear was dissipating increasingly.

One clear, cool autumn day, during a particularly fantastic solo surf session, I was sitting relaxed on the board after a fun, gliding wave, thinking about how effortless it felt to surf that day. Even though I had been out for an hour already and caught quite a few waves, almost nonstop the whole hour, I did not feel at all tired. And each wave I was privileged enough to engage felt effortless too. Paddling into the rolling water took little muscular effort, as I could now read the waves better. Popping up onto my feet felt smooth and natural; positioning my stance on this nine-foot-long glassy beauty became more instinctive. Even though I was surfing more in each session, I was doing it with less effort, so I wasn't getting tired like I had in the beginning.

This is economy of motion. Effortless effort. In today's terminology, more bang for the buck.

I had spent most of my life using a lot of effort to get little payback. Now I was understanding that the less effort I used, the more reward I got and the more energy I had to enjoy that payoff. With all of my typical Western exercise experiences, I became very tired afterward, whether it was running, weights, biking, basketball, circuit training, aerobics, or even some yoga classes. I used a lot of effort to get my body to work through these things. Now I understood that I could exercise my body without much effort, and instead of getting tired from my activity, I had more energy than when I started. Now that's the kind of exercise I want: one that makes me healthier and leaves me refreshed and renewed rather than exhausted and spent. I want to feel better, not worse.

Just because "no pain, no gain" rhymes doesn't mean it makes sense. Think about it. We spend our whole lives trying to get away from pain. Not only do we use a plethora of drugs and surgeries to try to escape pain, we also use alcohol, relationships, jobs, activities, social groups, and more to try to get away from what ails us, be that physical, mental, or emotional pain. We spend a huge amount of money on medicine, activities, and professionals that all say they will rid us of our pain. So does it make sense for us to seek pain in our quest to heal and become stronger? To me it doesn't. I now know there are ways to become stronger, healthier, and happier without self-inflicting pain. Tai chi and surfing were teaching me economy of motion, how to use less and get more through mindful movement and conscious choice making.

When I let go of my muscles, I feel the energy of the universe flowing through me in my tai chi forms, just as I feel the cosmic chi of a wave stoke my fire from a good ride. I am renewed, rewarded, and revived by letting go and allowing the energy of the activity to move me, as I try to dance with it, not control it. This physically letting go has allowed my mind to open to new possibilities, for it is only when I pour a little out of my cup that more can come into it.

Years ago, I never would have entertained the idea of renting out rooms to strangers on a near-nightly basis. People I didn't know coming and going from my house when I wasn't there (and when I was there)—that idea would have terrified me only ten years ago. The possibility of getting ripped off, of getting sued, of getting hurt in some way was too big a what-if for me.

Now, with a few years of surfing and tai chi having taught me to let go, I have loosed some fears I didn't even realize I had until I released them. With my first three guests, I realized how inflexible and stuck in my ways I had become. Each guest left the kitchen clean and tidy, but they didn't do it the way I was used to, nor did they put things back where I would have. This tiny thing upset me because, in my mind, they weren't doing it right.

Fortunately, I quickly realized how utterly stupid and rigid this was, and I let go of this ridiculous expression of my need for control and my instantaneous judgment of "wrong" instead of just a unique way to accomplish the same thing. Instead of potential trouble from strangers passing through my home, now I see fellow travelers looking to explore the unknown and my ability to support myself by assisting them. Letting go of my fear and preconceived ideas allowed me to simply live, to pay my bills while helping others. How very freeing to have left my former comfort zone of fear!

Thanks to tai chi and surfing, this metaphoric letting go has happened in many aspects of my life. When I let go of my desire for more and see that it will come (it must in the natural cycle of balance), then I let go of my struggle and find peace. I release my attachment to outcome, and my stress fades into the distance like a vanishing sunset. I become totally free: free of the future, which I know will come; free of my past—staying full of old, sour wine doesn't allow fresh wine to fill me—free to simply be here now. Now I can accept the current circumstance, knowing that if I want to, I can change it, or I can wait patiently to see what the Tao brings me next. Usually when I am patient and wait, what the Tao brings me is better than I ever expected or would have thought of myself. I learn to let go, to drift in the sea. I learn to wait for the next wave; and if it's right for me, I ride it to the best of my ability, connecting with the energy that comes my way and making the most of it, hoping to enjoy the ride and get stoked or tumbled. The fun is in the not knowing. That's the adventure of surfing the Tao.

In my letting go, drifting with the Sea of Chi, flashes of personal insight would now come to me while sitting relaxed on the board between waves. Before surfing, I only had these meaningful moments of self-awareness when I was able to calm my mind in moving or still meditation. It was in these gaps between thoughts that astounding information poured into my awareness, altering my perceptions of myself and reality.

Many great innovators and thinkers have confessed that their paradigm-shifting ideas came as flashes of insight, complete and whole in their conception when first entering their minds. Steve Jobs claimed the iPhone idea came to him during a profound meditation. Einstein wrote that he used "mind experiments," inducing meditative drifting, and from them received his perception-altering ideas. Nikola

Tesla claimed his ideas came to him while in a deep dream-like state. Srinivasa Ramanujan saw groundbreaking mathematical formulas, many of which are so advanced mathematicians cannot yet comprehend them, during his meditations. There are many such examples in every academic field throughout history.

When I let go, I feel as though I tap into a greater circuit of being, knowing and understanding, a more profound experience of life itself, as though I expand beyond my physical boundaries. Now that I was learning how to let go a little on the surfboard when bobbing about in the buoyant, playful ocean, I had more surf insight. I saw the parallels of learning to stand in surfing, tai chi, and life. How I stood on the board was a huge part of how well I maneuvered myself with the wave. How well I stood on my own feet in my tai chi form dictated if I could stay balanced and flow through the upper-body movements; how well I stood also determined if pain was part of a still qigong meditation. I observed how my lower body affected my upper body. If my stance was off, so were my arms and torso. When I think of the human body as a structure or building rising from the ground, I understand that if the building's foundation is not level or is unstable in any way, then the entire building above will be stressed and weaken unnaturally over time.

It is the same with our structural bodies, and it all starts with how we stand, sit, and hold ourselves. Posture plays a big part in how the human building degrades and in our overall health and well-being. Natural symmetry is key when standing, sitting, and moving. My grandma's sage advice to "sit up straight so you can think better" went way over my head when I was ten.

One of the most basic tai chi stances, called the bow stance, is the same as we stand when surfing: one foot out in front, facing forward; back foot angled out about forty-five degrees, with about hip width between them. This is the way an archer would stand when shooting a bow and arrow—that's where the name bow stance comes from. With the feet in a bow stance, one can move in multiple directions: forward and back, side to side, a full squatting position, or a high upright stance.

However, if the feet are ill positioned, either on the ground or the surfboard, it becomes more challenging to squat down, shift one's weight forward or back, or to turn the waist fully; all of which make both tai chi and surfing look less than polished and refined, and sometimes result in wipeouts on the surfboard. On stable ground, it's much easier to reposition an ill-placed foot than when trying to adapt to standing on a lilting, turning, tumbling platform while in the ocean.

Footwork became more critical to my surfing now that I had learned how to stand and was learning how to maneuver on the wave, to turn in various directions instead of being completely at the whim of the wave, like when I was a total grom in a wide, planted stick-bug stance. If I popped up on the board and didn't place my front foot wide enough, I couldn't easily push forward down the face of the wave to catch it and then shift weight to the back foot to stall the board or slow it down to match the speed of the slowly breaking curl. If I popped up with my feet too wide apart, I found my legs too stretched out to shift my weight or change my position in any way. This stance is what's called "stick-bug stance." And that's exactly what it looks like: legs too far apart; arms wide and usually in the air, resembling a praying mantis that's trying not to move so it isn't noticed. On the surfboard though, it's quite noticeable as an awkward position where the surfer has little control of the board and is just stuck there on it like a stick bug at the mercy of the wave's energy.

In a flash, I realized this learning-to-stand aspect of both surfing and tai chi had slowly taught me, and was still teaching me, self-responsibility in the world, and it was all perfectly metaphorical with life itself. Sitting there, drifting on my board in the ocean, I could see it all unwinding together: my human life, tai chi training, and surfing were parallel spiraling waves of energy growth.

Before I learned to crawl, I was carried about in my parents' arms, every aspect of my existence taken care of by them. I was vulnerable, frail, and unable to care for myself. I couldn't choose which way to go or even how to move. As a human being, and then as a surfer, I had first learned how to crawl. Starting out surfing at forty years old, it was not an easy, smooth, graceful transition from lying down flat on the surfboard to standing up with my feet flat on it. I would catch the wave, push myself up onto my hands and knees, swing out one leg so I had my front foot flat, and then push myself up with my hands to stand on both feet. I felt like I was crawling up the board to get on my feet.

It's like this with tai chi at first too. Before tai chi, I was unaware of my feet touching the ground and I moved through space haphazardly, mindlessly, carried about by the whims of the world directing and holding my attention. When I first started tai chi, I had to relearn how to move, becoming aware of myself and my impact on the world as my foot touched it with each slow step. It's quite challenging to put one's foot down softly and under control with little muscular effort. Even in my early twenties when I began tai chi, I was clumsy at first, clomping my feet, trampling about for several months before I could lightly place my heel down, roll my whole foot flat, then put weight on it.

In the first crawling stage of learning to stand on my own feet, I became oriented with the space around me, be it the crashing wave or my parents' living room. I learned how to put my feet flat, and with practice and some luck in the beginning, I could pull myself up onto my feet. I could stand on my own after a little training. Once I got my feet flat, I often just fell right over, not only as a toddler but also as a grown forty-year-old grom. On the surfboard I would finally crawl my way to my feet and then, plop, fall over onto my side into the ocean. It took me quite a bit to simply be able to stand and not fall over. I had to train my muscles to just hold me up in the world, be that the water world or the walking human world.

Once I got my feet planted and could hold myself upright in the topsy-turvy world, then I had to be able to hold my balance there, to just stay upright. I learned how to support myself. Once I became strong enough, I then learned how to stand more upright, instead of bent half over, head facing down, like a toddler observing what lies below as she gets ready for the inevitable fall. Standing upright more confidently now, I could see around me instead of just immediately beneath my feet. I could see around the room or around the wave and determine which way I wanted to go. I started to control my own momentum—on the wave and in life.

I learned that I didn't have to just go straight forward with the rush on incoming energy, I could ride the energy wave in different directions. I could follow my journey down many different paths. In tai chi training, I learned to align my head (intellect), heart (emotions), and belly (gut instinct), the three major *dan tiens*, or energy centers, in the body. I learned how to keep them in line with each other no matter which way I turned because my feet were firmly rooted into position on the ground. When I kept this alignment, even if I stood on one foot with the other extended to the side in a kick, I did not fall over. When I wasn't rooted down and in alignment with myself, I fell over.

Isn't this the way it is in life too? When we ignore the gentle yin wisdom of the heart and follow only the yang intellect of the mind, we easily fall out of balance. Once I learned how to keep myself together in alignment, then I had to make some choices. With my head up and eyes open, I could see the clear path in the living room and decide to try to walk toward Mom. Or I could see which way the wave was breaking and try to steer myself and my board in that direction. Learning to go in a direction took a lot of time. I had to not only control how my feet touched down, but also control my alignment, coordinate hundreds of muscles to propel me in that direction, and learn to balance the momentum so the energy of movement didn't push me ahead so fast that I lost balance and fell forward or got too far in front of the power of the wave and lost it. Learning to coordinate 635 skeletal muscles, all in harmony with gravity and momentum, takes time on land and even more time and practice on water.

Then, when I could stand with my head upright so my heart was open, I slowly learned how to steer my own course. I learned that by shifting my weight to my front foot on the surfboard, I put more weight near the front of the board and drove the energy forward. When

I put more weight on the rear foot, the board slowed down or sank into the wave. Depending on how precisely I shifted my weight forward or back, I would lose the wave, stay in harmony with it, or drive myself forward too fast and lose that power point of the wave's energy, which stayed behind me.

In life it is the same. I breathe and I learn how to crawl, how to stand, how to move, and how to direct which way I want to go; and with any luck, I'll learn how to read the changing tides and waves of energy that roll through life, so I can ride them with effortless effort. Hopefully, I learn as I grow to take care of myself in the world so that I don't have to be carried by others. In the ocean of life, while we may be out in the water with others, it's up to us to save ourselves, to take care of ourselves and our world. How efficiently we do it depends on our ability to see where we've put ourselves in the lineup in relation to the job or life partner or whatever energy may be rolling in. Will our timing and position be right to catch our dream job? It's up to us to make it happen, to position ourselves in line with the flow.

Every surfer knows that once you step foot in the ocean, it's up to you to take care of yourself. Even though there may be other people in the water with you or on the beach, it could take quite a while before anyone really noticed if you were hurt, facedown in the water. When the waves are breaking it can be difficult to see what's going on in the rolling, heaving reflective water. Even when someone does notice you need help, it may take some time for them to get to you. There's quite a bit more resistance when traveling through water than on land. It takes longer to get from point A to point B. As a surfer in an unpredictable ocean, I must be able to rescue myself instead of relying on someone to come to my aid. If I get tangled in fishing line (as I have) or kelp, or held underwater for a long time, only I can resolve the situation out there in the ocean. This really is the self-responsibility of survival.

On several separate occasions I've found myself in self-rescue mode even in a seemingly calm Atlantic Ocean. Two of these times were when the waves got bigger while I was already out. On a mild early-summer day, I found myself enjoying a lovely little waist-high morning surf session with a few of my surfing neighbors nearby in the water. Forty minutes had passed with the ocean delivering smooth, little easy-riders about two to three feet high when standing at the bottom of the wave. While waiting for another wave of galactic chi to roll my way, I noticed a change in the strength of the current. In an instant, it got much stronger beneath me. The next wave to come was much larger than those before, but still not overhead. It was a nice, smooth wave, so I went for it and caught a fun ride, then managed to turn out of the wave, lie down, and paddle back out for another.

Sitting on the board now, totally stoked by the last chest-high ride, I saw in the distance that the waves were getting consistently bigger. I paddled out a little farther into the ocean to let this larger set pass through while I waited for another smaller set that I was sure would come. It didn't come. In fact, the waves just kept getting bigger and bigger until they quickly became overhead in height, all within a matter of seven minutes. Now I knew I needed to go in to shore, as this was beyond my skill level. The most difficult part of the entire session was getting back to the sandy beach without catching what I saw as a monster wave and getting crushed by the huge walls of white water. My stroke quickly turned into anxiety and fear. With some hairy but careful timing between waves, I made it in without issue, my heart racing like a deer evading a hunter. I stood on the beach for a while calming my breath.

Looking out at the much larger waves from the safety of shore, my anxiety was replaced with a sense of accomplishment. I was proud of myself for recognizing that I needed to go in and doing so quickly and without getting hurt. I was happy that I had been blessed with such a great session, and as I carried my big board under my arm back to the boardwalk, I realized that if I had gotten clobbered by a big wave and been held down, it would only have been myself who could have saved me. A sense of confidence filled me, knowing I could take care of myself even in shifting, changing conditions. I was finally learning how to face everything and rise.

Being a surfer necessitates being self-responsible. Practicing tai chi does this also, as it makes us responsible for how we move in the world in a very literal way. Unfortunately, this is something we are no longer held responsible for: how we move our bodies. I'm sure there are many examples of this, but I can think of a big one that was in the news a few years back. In 1994 a New Mexico woman sued a McDonald's restaurant for getting burned by the hot coffee that she spilled on herself. She won the lawsuit. Other examples include people suing stores for tripping over steps and curbs. Is the store responsible for how your muscles move? Truly this is irresponsible thinking, and the most disturbing part to me is that frequently those who fail to monitor and control their own bodies are winning judgments!

Let's put this into perspective. A third party is being held responsible for how your body moves. Do you want a third party to be responsible for how your body moves? Think about this a moment. Let it sink in. When we continue to condone in our legal system these acts of irresponsibility of bodily control, we set a standard for the legal system to determine for us how to care for and move our bodies. This easily leads down an eerie, Orwellian path where a free society should not want to go, where the state mandates and controls diet and exercise as well as things like forced medication (which is happening in the world of vaccines).

Do you believe in bodily self-responsibility? Most women would say they have the final say over what happens within their reproductive bodies, but many of those same women won't take responsibility for lifestyle-induced type 2 diabetes. If we can't control our own bodies—with which we have the most intimate of all connections throughout life—how can we be trusted to drive a car? Oh, wait, that right could be on its way out too, as several companies are pouring millions into perfecting the self-driving car. We're being told this is partly to help reduce accidents caused by driver error; in other words, to protect us from ourselves.

Yet it's up to each of us to be responsible for controlling our own bodies. It's up to the individual to determine if his foot needs to come up higher to go over the curb. If the chili peppers are too hot for you, don't order them. If you get faint in the heat of summer, don't go to the Caribbean in August. If you're diabetic, stay away from the dessert bar. Watch where you're walking or driving instead of your phone, so you don't collide with a curb. This is simply taking responsibility for one's body, just as taking a small step forward with little to no muscular effort within a tai chi form is learning to control one's own body. And it's the same when we learn to keep our balance and stand up on a surfboard that's rocking and rolling and moving like water. These lessons of tai chi and the lessons of surfing are the same, and they are transferable to ordinary daily life.

We breathe. We learn to crawl. We learn to stand. We learn to move. We learn to choose for ourselves. Hopefully, we'll make good choices. If not, we remember the wipeout, and with enough experience we (hopefully) learn from our mistakes. Unfortunately, if we never experience the consequences of the wipeout, we don't learn. If we instead are rewarded for not taking care of ourselves, then we will want to fall again and again and again. I do not go seeking the pain of the fall, but when I get it, I experience it fully so I can learn from it and hopefully grow into making more responsible choices so I don't fall again. When I fall now, I try not to whine and cry about it, seeking attention for my mistake, some kind of reward. Many people fall into this trap unknowingly. I sure did not all that long ago, before I knew it was my own fault for falling. It's easy to complain about the traffic when we ourselves are in it and creating it.

The tai chi player is one who attempts to effortlessly control his own body, his own thoughts, and his own energy, and so is the surfer. Through the study of tai chi chuan and surfing, we start to take personal control of ourselves instead of handing that control over so we don't have to deal with self-responsibility. We go with the flow of the current, but we do so with full awareness of our choices and actions. We learn to control our own body and thus ourselves. This self-responsibility is echoed in the ways of nature. A lion cub does not blame its mother that it fell out of the tree, nor does it blame the tree it fell from or the ground it landed upon. This self-responsibility is a particularly useful and valuable skill not only for the individual but also for society as a whole. I think self-responsibility was what the founding fathers of the United States had in mind for our country. We've gotten lost along the way. We've lost our balance.

One of the reasons George Washington was revered by his countrymen was for his war conquests as a general, but it was his great concession that set him above all the rest. Even though the entire country would have been happy to see him stay in the White House as president, he chose to yield power and step down from the US presidency. He chose the yin way, to yield power and afford someone else the opportunity to steer the country's course. He did not choose self-aggrandizement and personal power, which some of our current world leaders seem to thrive on. Instead, he chose the power of the people to rule themselves freely. Indeed, society has gotten lost in the yang of *doing* and neglected the yin of *being*; imbalance has resulted.

In the same drifting, floating, encompassing mist of insight, I see how when the yang becomes full in our taiji symbol, when the white part is at its largest, it then slowly turns into yin; a thin line of black grows larger and larger. Once things have gotten as full as they can, then they start to empty. This is now beginning to happen on a societal scale, and many people are experiencing and recognizing a shift in traditional paradigms, pointing us to a new way of living that makes more sense. The influence of yin energy is slowly re-emerging once more as we witness the fullness of a yang-dominant world. Women (considered yin) are marching for rights in countries where they are oppressed. For the first time in history, women are now allowed to drive in all Middle Eastern countries—that is, in every country on Earth—finally. Because there are now women in political and media positions, female voices crying out from abuse are now being heard worldwide, evidenced by the explosive #MeToo movement.

The creative yin way is once again being recognized as necessary for progress, including within the realms of science and technology. Less static work places are becoming more popular, even garnering praise for flexible human-centered practices like work sharing, flexible scheduling, work-from-home options, daycare options, and, most noticeably, a much less rigid work dress code, overall. Yin is slowly coming back to create more balance. But we must be mindful to not let it overrun the yang, as can easily happen in a backlash effect. Yin is not superior to yang, just as yang is not superior to yin. When both work together in harmony, balance is achieved and harmony is found.

The current American undertone is one of division and opposition, which has infiltrated all levels of our times. White supremacy has reared its ugly head, pointing out a still-huge sense of division for one subset of our species toward another. The Democrat-versus-Republican political rift is coming close to mirroring the fervor last felt by the Whigs and Tories, with each party disparaging the character of the other and even threatening jail time and political ruin. The socioeconomic divisions are becoming more blatant, as "the haves" have more than ever in history and "the have nots" are working full-time jobs but still having to sleep in their cars or on the street every night because many simply can't afford even the necessity of shelter. Some people have become so disillusioned with religion that they've rebounded into anti-religion and feel free to scorn the beliefs of others openly while defying acceptable societal moral conventions. By seeing separation between us, we are choosing to emphasize our differences instead of working together to build a strong, healthy United States.

Yet hope awaits in the natural order of things. Once something like polarity has reached its highest division, the inevitable consequence is that things will merge together again. High tide always moves eventually into low tide.

United we stand, divided we fall. It's really that simple. It is up to us as individuals to stay in balance, walking the center line between yin and yang to stay in harmony instead of opposition; to be self-responsible. When we make balanced, responsible personal choices, our society becomes more balanced and our country can be united once more. When our citizens are balanced and healthy, our country will be balanced and healthy. We are our world. All is one. This is the heart of the Tao. This very notion is also surprisingly found at the heart of in- novative physics. In some ways, it seems the mystical and scientific are beginning to see how much they have in common, while both struggle to answer the same timeless human questions: Who am I? Where did we come from? What is the meaning of all this? The physicist and the master are no longer in opposition but now coming into harmony and *universal understanding*.

The form of the formless,
The image of the imageless,
It is called indefinable and beyond imagination.
Stand before it and there is no beginning.
Follow it and there is no end.
Stay with the ancient Tao, move with the present.
—*Lao Tzu, Tao Te Ching*

The flash of insight I had blew open my yang Western-educated mind like a riptide, blasting away and pulling out what no longer served me, bringing in a surge of fresh energy. Increased awareness came to me of the parallels between nature, surfing, tai chi, Tao, science, society, cosmology, and interpersonal relationships and how it all turned around the balance between yin and yang. I laughed aloud realizing the Tao is the Way. Stay with it to move with the present. I smiled, splashing the water around the surfboard with my hands gleefully as a child, my spirits lifted. While the water fear was still ever present, it was now simply an underlying presence instead of the center of attention. I was becoming too immersed in the field, the ocean, the Tao, to give my precious energy to this annoying, ridiculous fear.

With years of experience in the water now, my reality had taught my rational brain that there really was extraordinarily little chance of getting seriously hurt out here if I observed what was going on around me and acted in responsible accord. As I was adrift in the ocean, my mind now felt open to the flow of its ever-moving energy. Here, on the coastal Atlantic, even when there are no waves and the water is still and glassy on the surface, an ever-shifting energy lies below. This is formless and imageless. This energy cannot be painted into a landscape, but it is quite real.

It shifts and flows like a cloud of birds or shadowy school of fish; made up of individual aspects but flowing as a unified whole from the single organism into the universe. For the tai chi player and the surfer, the mind leads the energy; energy centers, or *dan tiens*, lead the individual parts of the body, hands, and feet; and the individual parts of the body lead the entire being, flowing in synchronistic, perfectly balanced whole.

This intangible field of energy seething within the ocean contains everything within the ocean yet is not the things that are held within it. As a mathematician might put it, the set cannot contain itself. The energy of the ocean is felt by the bird, whale, sailboat, starfish, and myriad other things, connecting them all together within a single unified ocean. In tai chi this is sometimes referred to as the Sea of Chi. In physics it's called the unified field. These concepts are interchangeable. A vast field of energy containing and uniting all within it. As a surfer, I see how the ocean unites us all. I pick up trash in and along the ocean that has writing in languages I do not know and couldn't even name. I see the debris of faraway storms in the waters surrounding me. I pick up debris from a cargo ship that went down in the Caribbean weeks ago. I have felt and seen oil and tar in the water and on the beach when there was an oil spill hundreds of miles away. I have a first-person, personal encounter with the reality that what one person/country/

company does on the other side of the world influences me because we are united by the Sea of Chi. We are all one within an imageless, undefined, indefinable morphing field of energy.

Einstein expressed that he believed our idea of separation between entities was a delusion, that we are all interconnected within what we now call the unified field, when he said, "A human being is a part of the whole. . . . He experiences himself, his thoughts and feelings as something separated from the rest—a kind of optical delusion of this consciousness. This delusion is a kind of prison, restricting us to our personal desires and to affection for a few persons nearest to us. Our task must be to free from this prison by widening our circle of compassion to embrace all living creatures and the whole of nature." How one of us treats the field, or whole of nature, can and more importantly does affect us all.

This is expressed in the nonlocal aspect of quantum mechanics. A measurement in one part of the field can be influenced by something in a distant part of the field, and the correlation between these two distant points happens faster than the speed of light. So, the very mechanics, the details of how our universe works, indicates there is an unseen connection between all things; the energy of all things is nonlocal; it reaches out farther than one fixed point and affects the entire energy field. The very basis of quantum mechanics says that what I do in my own personal life has a ripple effect out into the unified field and affects everything. Tai chi and Taoism teach us to be merciful, kind, and tolerant of others, as we are all related; an idea found in many societies and numerous spiritual traditions as well.

With more people and more media outlets in the world, we are starting to connect the dots that one country's nuclear meltdown into the ocean affects the fish and water quality worldwide. Industrial air pollution from unregulated countries wafts across borders, affecting the health of others. An oil spill in one isolated platform can affect the entire fishing industry in the Gulf of Mexico. One contaminated piece of factory equipment not properly sterilized can cause serious health issues in distant countries where that contaminated packaged food is consumed. What we do in our personal lives does affect each other, whether we choose to acknowledge that reality or ignore it. Even though we may perceive our lives as separate, isolated, pertaining only to ourselves and our immediate surroundings, our choices affect our field and our world, making our personal decisions nonlocal, in quantum terminology.

For instance, it may not seem like buying the cheapest pair of shoes for my kids affects world health, but it does. In the United States, the consumer, especially a cash-strapped parent, will typically opt for the least expensive of all options, regardless of anything else. So, Mom may buy the discount shoe store off-brand shoes labeled Made in Indonesia or China or Pakistan. Now, Mom loves her kids and would never think of doing harm to her own or anyone else's children. But her very frugal purchase of two pairs of cheap tennis shoes just helped make it possible for child factories to stay open and running in unregulated countries.

If a product seems too cheap for what it is, like a pair of shoes that costs less than a single meal, there may be something unpleasant along the supply chain making that product cheaper than it should be. Yes, Mom, by buying the cheapest shoes possible, you've just helped keep an unsafe child-labor factory in business so some profiteering, unscrupulous adult can live more luxuriously. Your life is nonlocal. This is the nature of the universe.

So if you think that what you do, buy, or throw away doesn't matter in the grand scheme of things, this actually contradicts the very laws of the universe. As we begin to grow up as individuals and a species, we begin to realize that simply ignoring knowledge doesn't make the truth go away. Our everyday choices have far-reaching consequences in the world, especially when enough of us make that same choice.

This leads directly into string theory. This physics theory is named for the effect one violin string vibrating has on all others. Though not touched, the other strings begin to vibrate as well, just by picking up the vibrating energy of the single plucked string. This is true for us and is easily seen in the transference of our emotional energy. If I'm mad and enter a calm, peaceful room, strangers in the room may turn and look at me, sensing my entry has changed the vibe of the room. I've seen firsthand numerous times how the stressed, fearful energy of an anticipated hurricane can cause panic in others. Often, when a massive storm is on its way to our Florida locale, there's an almost tangible fear and dread through the entire region. Stress, fear, and panic have a cascading effect as their vibration travels through the field of energy we all share. The more stress and fear I allow into my own personal life, the more stress resonates through my entire community.

Fortunately, string theory also applies to the harmonious vibrations of our fellow humans. This is shown in study upon study of how group energy affects the entire planetary field. In fact, human emotions influence the planet itself in a very real, measurable way. The HeartMath Institute has done some fascinating work in measuring the vibrations of the earth and how it is affected by humans. It's been known for some time that Earth vibrates at around 7.8 megahertz. This is known as the Schumann resonance, which, coincidentally, is measured using a combination of horizontal and vertical antennae. By correlating variances in the Schumann resonance at measuring stations throughout the globe, HeartMath Institute found two major changes in the planet's basic energy signature. One fluctuation was when the World Trade Center was attacked on September 11, 2001, and another fluctuation when Barak Obama was elected president of the United States.

The eyes of the entire world were captivated by these two historic events. This focus of mass human consciousness, or collective energy, tuned in with a united spirit of disbelief and sheer horror in one case and a collective focus on a vibration of hopeful change and optimism in the other, both manifested in a measurable change in the physical vibration of the planet Earth. This idea is echoed in the Princeton experiments that showed combined human thought influencing random event generators, something that was believed to be impossible: human thought changing how physical machinery operates. Our emotions and thoughts affect the physical reality of the planet, and this is now proven true. This is not some airy-fairy far-off, crazy notion; this is actual modern-day science confirming what the ancient Taoists like Lao Tzu said centuries ago. Stick with the ancient Tao, move with the present.

Not only do our thoughts and feelings affect the planet's health, they also affect our own personal health and the health of our families and communities. In the first study of tai chi at Folsom Prison, string theory, unified field, and nonlocal reality can all be observed in play. The study (now ongoing for over twenty years) showed that a small group of inmates practicing tai chi led to fewer repeat offenders and less unruly behavior overall within the prison. Interestingly, these effects are seen not just in the volunteering inmates that practice tai chi, but also in other inmates who do not engage in tai chi.

Simply by becoming mindful, calmer, and more centered in our tai chi practices, we affect the entire Sea of Chi and send a wave of healing energy to all around us. If simply practicing the gentle, slow-motion exercise of tai chi has this effect on prisoners and the entire prison environment, imagine what it does to us all when large groups practice together. We are all one. There is no separation. And when enough people together push energy to go in a certain direction, a wave is formed that ripples out and affects the entire population.

And what of time? If vibrations move through the unified field faster than the speed of light (our fastest unit of measurement), then time must exist in something other than a linear form. I thought about how time changes depending on what I am doing. We've all had the experience of five minutes seeming like an eternity when waiting for something. Too you've felt as though an entire day has gone by in a flash. The experience of time is a vastly different thing than the evenly spaced seconds ticked off by a precision watch at regular intervals. Sometimes time is fast. Sometimes it is slow.

The idea of linear time is outdated but is, unfortunately, still embraced by traditional yang establishments, including the American education system. The genius of Albert Einstein reasoned in the theory of relativity that time is relative to everyone based on how fast they are traveling. The only way I can wrap my nonscientific brain around this is to observe it in my own daily life. Even though the hours of the day tick by at the same rate on the clock, when I take the time to be still in qigong meditation or move very slowly in tai chi practice, my day slows down. When before my slow-motion practice, it seemed impossible to complete the list of to-dos for the day, somehow after moving slowly in tai chi, time seems to expand and I'm able to accomplish all that I need to that day. My slowing down has somehow created more time in my day even though the intervals on the clock don't show it. Time is relative to how quickly or slowly I move through my day. If I had not experienced the truth of this paradox for myself on many occasions, I would not believe it.

It's easy to get a swollen, heady feeling drifting out here in the oceanic Sea of Chi. The concepts are larger than I'm used to handling in my everyday life. Thinking about all this in large-scale proportions has an intoxicating effect on my brain, making me feel like I'm reeling. I try to bring it back down to a more basic scale for my small mind to digest. I look at the yin and yang of how our very universe and life exists. In particles, there must be both a positive and negative charge for activity to happen. Without polarization, there is only inertness; there is no flow between the two poles, each pulling on the other to cause electrical activity. Without both positive and negative, a battery has no charge. To my Taoist way of thinking, this is yin and yang. The simplest in form leading to the most complex in expression of movement.

Into my mind flows the idea that yin and yang are the driving force behind our computer technology. Without the simple binary code of zero and one, our current technology, which keeps expanding, would not exist at all. One and zero. Something and nothing. Yang and yin. Positive and negative. Male and female. Active and inactive. High tide and low tide. Ones and zeros. Without these simple, harmonious juxtapositions, nothing we know—no complex architecture, no art, no Internet, no society—none of it exists without the interplay of yin and yang.

As modern scientific instruments become more refined, they are starting to register more of the subtle energies of the universe. The energy, or chi, in the body can now be picked up by specific meters that measure energy fluctuations through contact with the skin. Even moving the measuring device one millimeter off an acupuncture point, where energy readings are high, drops the readings to almost nothing. The modern scientific understanding that so-called empty space is not empty has for millennia been understood as chi is always everywhere.

We know now too that intangible vibrating energy is what our physical world is built from, the solidity of all matter is an illusion, and that in the reality of our physical realm, subatomic particles, which make up the building blocks of matter, appear from nowhere and disappear again into the unknown. The physical building blocks of our physical world are not physical and simply appear and disappear. We do not know where they come from or where they go. We used to think that if we couldn't touch something, it wasn't real. Now we know, as physicist and author Dr. Amit Goswami has put it, "Consciousness, not matter, is the primary foundation of reality." What we think creates reality, and the universe itself is self-aware. This is high science, and it's the mystical as science starts to see the reality of the subatomic world better with a keener vision.

Einstein's famous $E = mc^2$ means everything is energy! If mass (m) is sped up to the speed of light (c) squared, then it becomes pure energy (E). When the vibration is higher, it's closer to pure energy. Understanding this concept, the ancient Taoists developed ways to enhance our biological vibration by clearing the energetic systems using the tools of the body: how we move (tai chi), how we sit, stand, and breathe (qigong), the thoughts in our minds (meditation), what we eat and drink (food healing), and our relationship to others and things around us (feng shui). This is what I call ancient biotechnology. These are the tools (technology) of the mindbody. They have been lovingly transmitted from the past yet will continue to heal us regardless of where one stands in time.

This ancient biotechnology is universally available to all humans no matter how rich or poor or what country we're from, because we all sit, stand, breathe, move, and think. The tools of the internal chi arts can be utilized by anyone wanting better balance, whether that harmony is sought in health of body, focus of mind, or raising of the spirit—also known as being in good relationship with the universe. Chi arts are subtle, ancient biotechnologies that adjust the subtle, unseen energy that is the very fabric of our physical existence. Is this science? Is it mysticism? Could science and mysticism simply be yin and yang perspectives of the same universal phenomena? Einstein may have been alluding to this thought when he wrote, "Science without religion is lame. Religion without science is blind."

The Vedic yoga systems, various Taoist qigong and tai chi systems, the Jewish and Christian traditions, and many First Nations traditions teach that we can raise our vibrations (our subtle, unseen energy, or chi) to have better connection to the Universal Mind, All There Is, Tao, collective consciousness, the unified field, by "going within." By raising our light/vibration/chi energy, we become healthier, more at peace, higher minded, and more balanced and connected to the natural world and even attain Enlightenment, which is a state of union with all, where we lose our delusion of separation.

As a young adult in my early twenties, I said and believed the words "All that chi energy stuff is a bunch of crap!" Now, after many years of tai chi, my brain can finally overcome its limiting "I need physical proof to believe it" left-brain thinking. My small mind can now comprehend the truth that all of us are conscious energy beings. Internationally acclaimed brain chemistry expert Dr. Candace Pert likened each of us to individual singular nodes on the interconnected brain of collective consciousness. I have no formal study of more than basic science from my years of Western education, but tai chi and surfing have given me the experience of what various sciences can only attempt to explain. Just as Lao Tzu told us at the very start, "The Tao that can be told is not the eternal Tao."

Modern science now also shares Taoist theories that there is no linear time or space and that it is possible to see/be in both the past and future as well as the present. The ancients of many traditions have told us that enlightenment comes from living in the moment, in the present. For myself, this is just one reason I practice the mindful movement that is tai chi. By simply moving through the complex motions, I am fully present in the now instead of analyzing my past and preparing for my future. Even if just for these few moments a day, I am here and now, fully aware of my mindbody, in the flow of the Sea of Chi. To me and millions of other tai chi and qigong practitioners, the future of our health care lies in the biotechnology of the past to keep us healthy in the present. "Stay with the ancient Tao, move with the present."

To acknowledge ignorance is wisdom.
To ignore knowledge is sickness.
To be sick of sickness is not sickness.
—Lao Tzu, Tao Te Ching

It was a Memorial Day weekend and the beaches were all crowded. They would have been even if the surf weren't good. But it just so happened that the surf was exceptionally good that slightly cool Sunday morning Mersea and I paddled out at Hightower Beach Park. The waves were clear, chest high, and trickling down off soft but powerful A-frame-shaped waves. Ah, perfect! Luckily, we got out early enough that there weren't a lot of people in the water yet. Mostly people come out later on Sundays; we were grateful. Learning to surf was teaching me to be more observant of the natural cycles that surrounded me daily.

It didn't take long for me to spot the many swirling schools of fish in the calm, glass-like ocean around us. I knew they had to be bigger fish due to the large wakes some were creating with their powerful tails and occasionally exposed dorsal fins. Since I could easily see these big schools, I was able to paddle away from them when they came my way. At first, I wasn't sure what kind of fish they were, and the waves were great, so I just dealt with the situation and enjoyed a few small, fun rides.

A little to our south a small pod of dolphins was also riding the waves. It seemed everyone was enjoying the beach that day. The group of bottlenose dolphins were slowly cruising north as they continued to ride wave after wave, swimming back out only to catch another ride in. They were having so much fun it showed in their multiple leaps in and out of the water, both riding the wave energy toward the beach and going back out for another. It was breathtaking to be so close to this amazing dolphin show. It also kicked in my fear full force.

Dolphins are beautiful to watch and because they seem to smile, appear friendly and cute. But I knew these dolphins each weighed three to five hundred pounds, sported about a hundred cone-shaped teeth to trap prey, could swim at speeds up to twenty-two miles per hour, and were more in control of what took place in the ocean than I was. These are meat-eating predators who rule their domain. I sometimes liked when there were dolphins out near me in the water because I had heard that when they are around, the sharks skedaddle.

But this pod of big dolphins was directly heading my way, and I was not finding them so cute or friendly. As a precaution, I caught a wave, rode it into shore, walked south down the beach past them, and paddled back out to enjoy the surf alongside them but with them now moving away from me, not toward me. Later Mersea commented that I'd get over that fear too one day. That sweet, soft Sunday-morning session, she surfed several waves with dolphins popping in and out of the wave right beside her, all of them laughing and smiling all the way.

When I paddled back out past the oh so terrifying dolphins playing, I paddled right into one of those other swirling schools of unknown fish. They were big. In fact, as some of them came partially out of the water as they pursued their smaller prey, they looked a lot like sea monsters: round and slimy with gray tentacle-like tubes undulating in and out of the water that were at least seven inches in diameter. Turns out it was the beginning of tarpon season, as it is every Memorial Day weekend, which took me a few more years to recognize.

The tarpon were big, at least five feet long, some longer, and a few of them brushed against me as I tried, panicking, to get out of the feeding school. I did push past them in a few paddle strokes, but time went too slow until I got clear of their hungry, churning mayhem. I scanned the ocean's surface to make sure I wasn't paddling into any more of them, so I could go sit, relax, breathe, and collect myself. I felt a bit like Dorothy in the *Wizard of Oz*: tarpons and dolphins and waves, oh my! I felt ALIVE! I felt vibrant, strong, in control of myself out here in the swirling ocean of life, waiting for what came next.

That day, it occurred to me that we need both a fast heart rate to stimulate us as well as the slower heart rate of calm and still. Just enough stress to push the system to grow and expand but not stay there, returning to the still to nourish and heal. I was grateful to have both yang and yin through surfing. There was no doubt that surfing and tai chi together were making me fitter, healthier, and more alive and vibrant now, over forty-five, than I was when I was running marathons in my early thirties.

According to a consensus among numerous Internet sources, the United States government spent about $3 trillion over six years on the war in Iraq. It's estimated that this year alone (2017), the United States government will pay over $3 trillion on our health care, the most expensive health care in the world! That's just one year of health care compared to six years of war!

In a review of online research, I discovered that the average American who has planned and saved for retirement will not be able to pay for her own medical expenses because the cost is skyrocketing while demand is also at an all-time high as the country's population is aging. When this happens, the government and health-care infrastructure absorb the cost and eventually must raise their prices and/or taxes because of it. It's estimated the US economy would save more than $10 billion if its citizens utilized tai chi for fall prevention, just one of tai chi's many proven benefits. In the end, we all pay for those who do not take care of themselves like responsible adults. There is a ripple effect through the entire field.

To me it only makes sense to practice the preventative health care of the traditional Chinese medicine known as qigong and tai chi. The prescription for this medicine is only twenty minutes a day. When I follow this prescription, I don't have the hassle or expense of preventable health problems. I feel better, and my mindbody functions better. This is cost effective: it keeps me healthy without going into the poorhouse. Fortunately, I'm not alone in this thinking. According to internationally recognized Doctor of Oriental Medicine Roger Jahnke, with the cost of mindbody practices being incredibly low, widespread use of chi arts can eliminate the health-cost crisis.

Thankfully, as a tai chi devotee and avid surfer, my health is rather good; at forty-five years old I take no prescriptions. But this is not the case for millions of Americans. If you've ever had family in the "health-care system," then you know how stressful and financially draining it can be trying to simply stay comfortable in one's body. Fortunately, there's a treatment modality out there that's been proven effective in study after study to improve numerous health issues and keep you out of the doctor's office to begin with. It's endorsed by the Arthritis Foundation as safe and effective; it's recommended by the Mayo Clinic, the Centers for Disease Control, the National Health Institute, Harvard Health, and numerous other trusted institutions. Thankfully, this treatment is cost effective: it saves you money on health care.

What if I told you this treatment is also proven to help reverse DNA damage and thus slow down biological aging? Would I have your attention then? Now let's pile on top of this huge list of benefits: improvements in mood, strength, balance, focus, fall prevention, improved cardiovascular function, stronger immune system, better digestion, normalized blood pressure, enhanced cognitive function, and the list goes on. One might think that a therapy that can do all this must have some bad side effects, but none have been found. We know it's safe because it's been studied and used for at least two thousand years. This wonder treatment is twenty minutes of daily tai chi.

As difficult as it may be to believe, these ancient mindbody exercises have been shown to help with all these conditions and many more, ranging from anorexia to Parkinson's. And yes, research has now found that tai chi and qigong even affect the very biological clock itself by reversing damage to the DNA's telomeres.

In 2008 the Nobel Prize for medicine was awarded to a group of scientists who discovered what they had named the telomere. The existence of the telomere had been known since the early 1980s but didn't become common knowledge until the 2008 Nobel Prize was awarded. The telomere has been called "the biological clock" by many scientists. I'm sure you know what DNA is: our biological blueprint or physical life plan. DNA is a long double spiral of chromosomes—our genes, which control our inheritable traits: eye color, predisposition to certain illnesses, skin color, body size, curly or straight hair, etc. At the ends of the chromosomes are caps that keep the strand from unraveling and deteriorating. These caps are the telomeres. The research team showed there's a direct link between age and telomere length. As we age, these telomeres begin to degrade and can no longer protect our DNA from unraveling into destruction. Dolly, the first sheep that was cloned, died prematurely because she ran out of telomeres. (Her DNA was taken from another sheep, which was already partway through its life and thus had deteriorating telomeres.)

The discovery of telomeres alone is major—Nobel Prize major.

Since the existence of telomeres was known to the scientific community since the 1980s, research had been done on them for years before numerous studies began to make it to the public in the early twenty-first century, right around the same time as the Nobel award.

In July 2008, Herbert Benson, who was the lead developer of the relaxation response concept, was among the researchers on a breakthrough study exploring the extent to which mindbody practices triggering the relaxation response can influence gene expression. The resulting research article was entitled "Genomic Counter-Stress Changes Induced by the Relaxation Response."

The authors stated that their study showed the relaxation response changed the expression of genes involved with inflammation, programmed cell death, and the handling of free radicals. Dr. Benson concluded that changing the activity of the mind can alter basic genetic instructions and how they are implemented. Our genes are no longer our fate, and the old excuse "it's in my genes" can no longer be used to shirk the self-responsibility of the care of our own health. If we can control our thoughts, we can control how our DNA acts.

Earlier, in February 2005, a similar study was completed that focused specifically on gene expression in qigong. It appears that intention-based practices that activate the relaxation response, specifically qigong in this study, can change how genes behave. The research showed that practices that induce the relaxation response (a specific, measurable, biological state), repair damage to the telomere. Researchers noted that this healing relaxation response is induced by practicing qigong, tai chi, meditation, gentle forms of yoga, and biofeedback techniques. Typically, what happens as we age is the telomere, which is shaped like a pyramid on the end of the chromosome, starts to degrade. When this happens, the chromosome—our physical life plan—is no longer protected and begins to degrade as well. This eventually leads to death. Only in the biological state of the relaxation response does the telomere heal and repair.

The implications are that individuals can purposefully shift genetic function to reverse programmed cell death. The traditions of both qigong and yoga theorize that these practices assist in an alchemical production of "the elixir" of longevity. You may be familiar with the so-called myths of Chinese immortals or Hindu yogis who live for hundreds of years, never growing older. The research we have seen suggests this elixir, or fountain of youth, is more than just a mythological legend. Now we have scientific evidence pointing us directly to it. This same evidence exclaims that the fountain of youth lies not in a cream or supplement, but it is already within us.

Mindbody practices that produce the relaxation response have been used by people across cultures for thousands of years to prevent and treat disease and generate states of mind that foster greater performance and intuitive insight. Only recently has science developed the tools to prove what qigong and tai chi practitioners have known for centuries: a calm mind and quiet heart lead to health and longevity.

The relaxation response has been proposed as the counterpoint to the fight-or-flight state—the stress response. Fight-or-flight and the relaxation response are like the yang and yin of each other. Numerous studies have shown that both the relaxation response and fight-or-flight have distinct profiles of physiological and gene-expression change. Over time fight-or-flight has degenerative effects on biological cells and systems, while the relaxation response has restorative effects on biological cells and systems and potentially the entire human organism. In other words, if you get super stressed out repeatedly enough times, it will *cause* cells and telomeres (and thus your body) to physically degrade, or age. If you engage in peaceful practices repeatedly enough times, it will heal and restore damaged cells and telomeres, thus healing and restoring you.

Research by the Harvard Medical School, the Mayo Clinic, and many, many others have proven that the practice of qigong positively affects gene expression, the immune system, the nervous system, and cellular function, allowing cells to live longer. This is true anti-aging and the legendary fountain of youth that springs forth from deep within us. Dr. Benson now concludes that genes that get altered or turned off by stress can be turned back on by invoking the relaxation response for about twenty minutes a day. It's like reverse thinking, or a yin-yang effect. If we can wreak havoc on ourselves with lifestyle choices, the reverse is also true: that we can heal ourselves using different options in these same daily choices. This is yin and yang at its finest: used to help and heal, not oppose and fight.

One of the best aspects of qigong and tai chi is that it's free medicine. Once I learn a little qigong or tai chi, it doesn't cost a thing to practice. There's no special equipment or clothes needed. Nothing to buy, no subscription necessary, and no pricey health club membership. I don't know about you, but I'm not made of money; so, to be able to use a treatment that's been shown effective for so many conditions for no money, that is indeed priceless.

Learning all this over the course of twenty years of tai chi and qigong practice has taught me that we are each responsible for our own health. If we can overcome even bad genetics using peaceful practices of mindfulness, then most of us have no excuse for poor health other than not being responsible enough to simply take care of ourselves. But if we don't take care of ourselves, who will? Your university-trained Western doctor? No; he'll write you another prescription and order another test or send you to a different specialist. Will your insurance company take care of you when you're unable to get out of bed? No; they might help you pay some of the bills, but they won't take care of you. In the end, we are all responsible for the health and well-being of the body we came with.

I think of my body as a car. My body is my vehicle to get around this life in. Just like my car, if I choose to put polluted, inferior products into my gas tank, eventually my engine will clog up and not work so well. If I let my car sit in the garage and never start it up or take it for a drive, in a short amount of time it will start to lose its battery life and won't perform so well when I do choose to use it. The more miles and years I have on my car (and my body), the more maintenance and care it's going to need to keep it going. I often see people at the corner car wash who obviously take better care of the car they'll only have a few years than of the body they must travel in the rest of their life.

Fortunately, many well-educated health-care professionals believe what the research shows: if we are self-responsible and do twenty minutes of tai chi or qigong a day, we will stay healthier as individuals, and therefore as a nation, resulting in an overall reduction in government spending on health-care interventions as well as improvements in our own personal quality of life. Author and tai chi expert Dr. Roger Jahnke calls himself a "health patriot" for this very reason. I now think of myself and everyone who practices and promotes tai chi and qigong as health patriots helping create a healthier, stronger America and world on many levels simultaneously.

The research has already been done, and it proves the efficacy of these mindful moving forms of meditation as true health care, not the disease care that our current system is. Western medicine has done little to care for health; it focuses on fighting dis-ease once it has already begun. That's not a health-care system; that's a disease-care system to take care of the disease instead of the health. This is a very yang approach, as is reflected in the very language of Western medicine: to *fight* a disease, to *battle* cancer. Western medicine often speaks and acts as though it's in a war with the natural ways of the mindbody and it's willing to sacrifice a lot of beneficial soldiers in that war. Western medicine is quite willing to kill one organ to save another. The side effects of all pharmaceuticals prove this. The medicine itself will often harm us.

Now, don't get me wrong. I'm not anti-Western medicine at all. If it weren't for the amazing advances in Western medical technology, I'd have only one leg instead of the metal that supports the right one and my dad's heart would have failed years ago without a successful cardiac ablation. Western medicine is fantastic for mechanical issues focused on the nuts and bolts of the physical body as well as for dealing with immediate trauma. Yet despite these fantastic medical advances, Western medicine, while miraculous at times, is also woefully inadequate at caring for the entire human, the whole person composed not only of body but also of mind and spirit. Western medicine is not holistic but segmented in its approach to health.

Chinese medicine is more nurturing in nature. First, it doesn't wait until it must "fight a disease"; instead, it fosters and boosts an already-healthy system so that it won't be susceptible to illness. If illness should come, instead of going to war, Chinese medicine looks to nurture that which is being depleted by the dis-ease, boost that which will naturally get rid of the issue, and starve the disease itself, depriving it of what it needs to thrive. This involves not just acupuncture, herbs, and elixirs, but also relationships and home-environmental situations that can be toxic and causing imbalance. A discordant home can cause dis-ease.

Acknowledging this whole-person, (w)holistic, style of caring for health, Chinese medicine doesn't focus solely on the body, as Western medicine tends to, but also addresses a person's mind and spirit, their nature or general predisposition. Surely you acknowledge that we need health of body, mind, and spirit to be vibrant and whole as human beings. Health doesn't just mean good blood pressure and cholesterol counts; it also means lightness of being in the world, not depression and anxiety. I know many people who, despite loving to work out hard in Western styles of exercise and looking fit and healthy on the outside with great doctor's reports, live full time on antidepressants due to anxiety and stress. This is not health. This is imbalance. To stress and beautify the body at the expense of the spirit is harmful in the end. We need balance of not only our physical health but also our mental health. When these two are in balance, our spirits are lifted; we become vibrant, full of vim, vigor, and vitality, full of chi or life-force energy—what is often referred to as having a lust for life.

Western health looks mostly to fortifying the outside, the body, the visible, tangible yang aspect of being. There's a saying in qigong and tai chi: strive to be steel wrapped in cotton. Make the inside of the body as strong as steel and the outside as soft and pliable as cotton, meaning the core should be strong and solid while the muscles and tendons should be flexible and relaxed. In Western culture there's a tendency to promote the opposite: make the outside of the body appear healthy, and if that looks healthy, the inside doesn't seem to matter. This is not in health or balance. This does not bring us back to wholeness.

What of the internal, invisible, intangible aspect of being? These are rarely even considered in the health of the whole being. While mental health is highly medicated in the United States, just mentioning that you're working with a psychologist, psychiatrist, or spiritual counselor creates an image of instability for most people because mental and spiritual health are somehow considered taboo to speak of in terms of health care. Coworkers may think better of you for going to the gym to keep the body fit, but the same people are likely to think there's something wrong with you if you tell them you're working with therapists on strengthening your mental or spiritual health. Just because we cannot measure, see, or touch a person's invisible spirit does not mean it's not important for overall health. Chinese medicine seeks to fortify from within instead of from without, building the yin, invisible spirit of a person to help the yang body heal.

Those who do not believe in spirit are missing the majority of all that exists in this shared reality: the unseen and unseeable. The millions of Americans like me who consistently practice tai chi and qigong have discovered that these traditional Chinese medicines will balance body, mind, and, yes, spirit, or the unseen energy we all possess whether we believe in that stuff or not. Even those who've only seen tai chi and never done it experience the truth in this spirit-calming effect. I often hear from strangers in the parks where I practice, "That looks so peaceful and meditative." The chi arts do indeed look as calming to the spirit as science has proven they are.

Should we always have a calm spirit? No, of course not. That too would be out of balance. Sometimes we need to be charged up, ready and willing to act defensively to simply survive in the world. Sometimes we need to get angry to speak up for ourselves when we've been taken advantage of. But to always be fired up, caffeinated, on call—this is most definitely out of balance. As biological creatures we also need to rest, rejuvenate, and heal. Yet how many people do you know who schedule time to do less? To heal?

Surely you know someone who schedules every minute of every day so that they can have more. Yet when it comes to scheduling even an hour a week to rest and heal, there's no hearing of it. Sadly enough, some people must be forced by their employers to simply use the vacation time they are allotted. You see, these people are the producers, the doers, the accomplishers with no time to waste, as they call it. They tend to follow the motto "I'll rest when I'm dead." Well, if this is you, you'll have plenty of time to catch up on that rest because you won't live awfully long if you don't let your body heal. When we push too hard, go too fast, and engage in those yang activities as our lifestyle, we stress our bodies, our minds, and our spirits, and our health usually fails in some way, making us take time to heal whether we want to or not.

Some interesting research has come out on stress and disease in the last ten to thirty years. To sum up what I've learned in perusing a great deal of it, stress CAUSES disease. Not contributes to, not influences, but outright CAUSES diseases such as hypertension, adrenal failure, autoimmune disorders, fibromyalgia, and a host of other modern illnesses that are on the rise in driven, yang-centric cultures. Other than being a victim of violence or an accident, nothing kills like stress. Stress: pushing too fast, too much, too hard, no rest, no time to heal, nothing but pressure in the mind and body. This is the spirit, the energy of a person, being out of balance. Engaging in the slow-motion, calming, healing chi arts allows the mindbody to rest, to slow down and simply be in the moment, instead of living in the future, stressing for more time, more energy, more money, or whatever it may be. The very nonproductive act of surfing can also have this calming, healing effect.

There's a great deal of medical research out there on the healing power of tai chi and qigong. It's easy to find on the Internet; an especially good tool is www.WorldTaiChiDay.org, which offers numerous free resources including links to a plethora of medical research on the chi arts. Even the very Western Harvard Medical School has done studies that show that engaging in the practice of tai chi on a regular basis makes one calmer and less stressed, producing fewer stress hormones and boosting production of serotonin. Thus, it helps balance the unseen energies that influence the spirit. Don't just take my word on it, check out the research for yourself. There are loads of scientific evidence for the efficacy of the chi arts.

As for surfing, not so much. In fact, surfing is considered by mainstream society to be so frivolous that no research was conducted on its effects until the last five years. I hope I speak for surfers all over the planet when I say surfing is far from being a frivolous activity. As any surfer knows, when you've had a hard day or you're depressed or you have a problem at work, just being out in the ocean, breathing in the clean, oxygenated air and connecting with the energy of nature, just being out there—not even standing up on the board but just being in that shifting, watery yin world—will heal your spirit and raise your energy.

The United States Navy thinks so too. In fact, the navy is so interested in using surfing for post-traumatic stress disorder and depression that in 2008 it started a surfing program at the San Diego Naval Medical Center. The one-million-dollar project is studying how surfing affects veterans suffering from PTSD, sleep disorders, anxiety, and depression. So far, the results lead to the conclusion that surfing can help heal in all these areas. And if it can help heal the wounded, why can it not help push the healthy further?

When out on a surfboard, depression fades. The spirit is calmed and energized, refreshed and renewed. Out here the mindbody energy must leave all else behind and be engaged in the now, not the past or future. Because surfing is nonproductive, a yang, production-centered world mistakes it as frivolous and sometimes juvenile or irresponsible, when in fact, it can be the balancing factor in someone's life.

Yet surfing, even gentle surfing, is rightly considered an extreme sport. Every single time a surfer paddles out into the ocean she takes her life into her own hands; she takes ultimate responsibility for herself. It is dangerous, even in knee-deep water, to engage the ocean. I've seen huge two-hundred-plus-pound men swept off their feet in shin-deep water. Every year there are numerous drownings along the coast of Florida, usually people not using their heads, making poor choices. Surfing in unpredictable ocean water is dangerous, and because of that the surfer must let everything else go and be present in the moment simply to survive in the water.

Am I in an appropriate position to catch the most powerful part of the wave? How is the wave forming, and is it a wave I want to engage? Are there any schools of fish heading my way that might draw larger predators toward me? And it just goes on and on to the point that the surfer simply is, right now and right here, aware and in the moment without thinking about any of it. This alone, in our very future-based society, is a spirit-calming act. To simply be right here, literally immersed in nature, right now, translates into no stress about the family or the job or money. Just awareness of being. This alone brings balance to our spirits, our unseen energy that's often utterly consumed with achieving instead of healing, *doing* instead of *being*, acting instead of observing.

While not everyone can live by the coast and surf, nor would everyone want to, everyone who wishes to heal themselves can easily learn a little tai chi and qigong, avoiding the dangers of surfing. It's so convenient now with many classes available online and thousands of YouTube videos devoted to the arts from enthusiasts all over the world. Healing arts are so much more accessible now than when I bought that first VHS Yang short-form video out of desperation to heal. The internal arts of tai chi and qigong are proven health-care systems that have been working for at least two thousand years, unlike the last one hundred fifty or so years of "traditional medicine." It seems obvious that the cost-efficient treatments of qigong and tai chi will be, and should be, playing a larger role in preventative health care and health maintenance. The key to the future of health lies in ancient biotechnology that does no harm. Even one of our brightest futurists, Thomas Edison, saw this when he wrote, "The doctor of the future will give no medicine but will interest his patients in the care of the human frame."

As I ponder these thoughts of health, surfing, yin, and yang, drifting in the sea waiting for waves of energy to roll my way, I feel connected to the unified field, as though I have understanding, wisdom, and knowledge beyond myself that does not come from me but from a larger, all-encompassing source. Could it be that in the unified field where we are all connected, we have access to all the information contained there? Is this the collective consciousness? Is this what some have called the Akashic Records, where all the information from human life experience is stored?

I drift with it, allowing my thoughts to flow as freely as the gentle currents beneath my surfboard. Letting go, allowing the yin flow without overanalyzing the thoughts as they drift in and out. Occasionally, when I look to shore from my buoyant perch beyond the breaking waves, I see balloon-like clouds of people rolling back and forth on the beach, in and out of the shallow waters. They are mostly round, especially in the tourist season. When I was a teenager and into my early twenties, it was unusual to see round people who had a challenging time getting in and out of cars or restaurant booths, not to mention beach chairs. Now these oblique people are everywhere and, often, the only people surrounding me. Big, round, roly-poly people who sadly don't know what it feels like to be tall, upright, and healthy, who don't understand the sheer joy of existence that can come from taking care of the body so it moves like a well-oiled precision machine. They don't know that a healthy body produces some of the most euphoric drugs on the planet and changes life entirely. Seeing the proliferation of round people, I feel sad for my country and my countrymen. I catch the next wave and the sadness dissipates, taken over by the joy of a small, glassy wave of healing cosmic energy.

I hope my neighbors have the self-responsibility and willpower necessary to care for themselves because, in the end, their very lives depend on it. The government won't necessarily take care of them; ask a veteran. The insurance company won't take care of them; ask someone who's experienced medical bankruptcy. Their doctors won't always be able to take care of them; the third-leading cause of death in America, according to the American Medical Association itself, is medical error. That means the "health care" system itself is the third-leading cause of death. In the end, we must rely on ourselves to keep our own bodies and minds healthy.

As it stands right now, we Americans are currently being held down by a system where we pay for our own dis-ease. To obtain health, we must start paying for health instead. We must reinforce what we want, not feed our energy into the dis-ease we don't want. What we pay for as individuals, we promote. Are we paying for our own health or our own dis-ease?

Some time back, a less than healthy family member chided me for spending more money on good organic produce than on health insurance. I pointed out that what I eat *is* my health and it's also insurance that I *keep* my health. Food is our fuel, and the cleaner it is the better our brains and bodies work. It just makes sense. If a pill smaller than the tip of your finger taken three times a week can significantly affect how your heart works, then what you eat every day obviously adds up to impact your long-term health. My wise grandma used to tell me, "You are what you eat, kid." I didn't realize at the time how right she was. To me it's worth paying more for quality food in the short term and feeling better for it in the long term. Pay for health, not dis-ease.

Unfortunately, this is not how "health care" is done in America, not yet anyway. This is part of our fear breath here, part of our health crisis. In America we have the world's most expensive health care but have consistently been ranked last in the developed world in the overall health of our citizens. One report on health in developed countries from CBS News states that "in comparing results from the other ten countries, adults in the United States are sicker and more economically disadvantaged." If we stop paying for bad "food" and unnecessary medications, many of the symptoms of our health crisis will simply go away. Yet we must also stop paying for those who refuse to take responsibility for even their own bodies. If we stop paying so much to support lifestyle-induced diseases, we can put that money into educating people to make smarter health-care choices. We need to stop feeding the dis-ease and start feeding and nourishing self-responsibility in health instead.

Genuine, old-fashioned self-responsibility typically comes through trials and tests of character and will. Self-responsibility was a driving force in the formation of America and its philosophy of rugged independence. Yet self-responsibility can rarely be found in a life focused on building comfort and profit, which dominates modern life here. I am still learning this pure love of self; learning to let go of that which doesn't serve me, that which is only a burden of ego and maintenance so that I can keep what does serve my highest good, not my greatest comfort.

Our current norms have our children stuck indoors behind screens that we know damage their vision. If we think our health is declining now, the future for our children's health isn't looking so good. We need to teach them there are more important things than comfort and that sometimes comfort can be downright bad for us. It wasn't until the advent of our many "modern conveniences" that the overall health of our country started to decline. In fact, looking into human history, our ancestors had less deterioration of their joints from natural causes than we currently have. Many orthopedic issues, it seems, are a modern, postindustrial phenomenon. Many of us have forgotten the value in "eating bitterness," in working hard for something and enduring challenges, and instead always seek the sugary sweets of the dessert. The Buddha states simply, "It is because of the mud that the lotus can bloom."

In keeping up with my ritual sunrise tai chi exercises on the beach, I choose to responsibly improve and sustain my own health and balance in the world. It is not comfortable or easy to take care of my mindbody. But I must. No one else will. So I get up early, usually long before the sun, I read *Tao Te Ching*, and I drink my morning tea, preparing consciously for the day. I walk over the now-empty A1A to the sandy beach; it's still too early for most automobile traffic. I must wait for only one specialty Longboard BrewHaHa delivery truck to roll by. I touch the earth with my bare feet, sinking into the still-cool sand. I breathe. I stretch. I start to move, slowly, mindfully. The skyline starts to illuminate in soft but majestic lavenders. The gentle sound of the lightly rolling ocean drown out any roadside traffic just sixty feet on the other side of the dune.

I stand still for quite some time; Holding Post the exercise is sometimes called. My arms are rounded out in front of me as if I'm hugging a big tree, and I stand still while breathing. I stand long enough to witness the subtle changes in the sky and ocean as the house lights come up for the day. I see early-morning, pre-work fishermen cast a few times on the shoreline nearby and then leave to go work. I see the beach runners first going one way, then the other before heading home to take the kids to school or whatever their day may hold. I stand and relax more. My posture straightens out a bit and my spine lengthens naturally as small areas of tension in my back, neck, and legs are slowly unwound by simply being still and consciously letting go.

As the bright golden disc of the sun emerges from the waters of the Atlantic, all beach movement stops. There is a pause as people turn from what they are doing to face the sun. A few bring out their cameras in a vain attempt to capture the majesty of the moment. A squad of pelicans hovers in a quiet mirage over a small ripple in the water, using the energy to propel their whole line north up the beachline. Another perfect moment. Time has stopped. Soon the beachgoers start moving again, doing what they need to get done. I alone am left standing after sunrise, the beach once again deserted until the midmorning senior sunbathers make their way out. This standing, breathing starts my day right. But it is not easy; rarely is it easy. Yet I am willing to stand, relax, and breathe knowing that soon after, the doing will once again begin.

By exposing myself daily to the soft but majestic wonder that is a beach sunrise and then walking back home across A1A through the diesel stench and metallic rush of morning traffic, I move through both the natural world and the man-made world, what is usually referred to as "the real world."

What is the real world? What is it to you? Can you describe it? How do you get along in the real world? What are the skills you need to survive there? Regardless of our physical surroundings, our perception determines our reality. Since we can choose to change our perception using various tools, we can choose to change our reality. What the real world is, is in fact up to the individual and their perception. Thankfully, surfing and tai chi have done an excellent job of keeping my real world attached to the natural world. Unfortunately, many people have lost that connection to the natural world, the world that 99.9 percent of all humans for thousands of years considered "the real world." Here's what I'm talking about:

The central east coast of Florida is a tourist hot spot, and it's easy to distinguish tourists from locals on the beach when you live here. This is an actual conversation between tourists on the beach and one that I've heard variations of many times: "This place is amazing. I wish I could stay. Yes, it's really too bad we have to go back to the real world." From the context, they mean they must leave the natural world of the beach and return to the work world, which obviously is more real for them than the natural world that humans have lived in for all of our recorded history.

Do you feel this way? Do you feel that the man-made world is the real world, as opposed to the woods, mountains, beach, or desert? If you want to, you can change this perspective. Just like the tourists on my local beach, if you want the beach life to be your version of real life, you can choose to make this happen. If you've ever experienced the moving power of a sunset or the heart-opening relief of a walk through an old forest, then you know how healing the real, physical earth can be. And now there's quite a bit of hard scientific evidence pointing out that being in the man-made world causes stress and dis-ease, while simply being in the natural world will heal the mindbody. As noted Zen philosopher Alan Watts reminds us, "You didn't come into this world. You came out of it. Like a wave out of the ocean. You are not a stranger here."

It's difficult to change from what we know as "normal" and widen our perspective of what is real and in so doing heal ourselves. I know how hard that change can be. It was extremely difficult for me to push myself past my fear of the water, but doing so widened my understanding of what it means to live in harmony with the world. It's just not safe to live surrounded by water and be utterly terrified of it. I left my comfort zone to overcome my fear. It's hard to leave our comfort zone, even when it may be killing us. Have you ever heard of the normalcy effect? It's remarkably interesting and may apply to your life in some way. I've found it a useful and humbling gauge in my own life. The normalcy effect occurs when an organism is exposed to an environment that changes so slowly over time that the organism doesn't notice the change and thinks everything is normal and remaining the same. When danger becomes imminent, the organism has become so complacent that it will not move out of harm's way.

Here's a perfect example of the normalcy effect: Put a bunch of live frogs (organisms) in a pot of room-temperature water and the frogs will mostly stay there. Put the pot on the stove and very slowly heat it up to a boil; the frogs will stay there and allow themselves to be boiled alive. The water temperature changes so slowly that it becomes the frogs' normal, and thus they do not jump out even though being boiled alive. If, however, you put a bunch of live frogs into a pot of already boiling water, they will jump right back out so fast it looks like they bounce off the top of the water. They know boiling water will kill them because it's not normal.

The same thing has happened to us humans, including my beautiful, strong countrymen. We are allowing our new "normal" and accepted ways of fast food, fast lives, quick fixes, sedentary stress, depressing 24/7 newscasts, overabundance of prescription medications, and little physical activity; we are allowing this new normal to slowly kill us. If we want to escape the unhealthy that is the new normal, we simply must become self-responsible.

It's difficult to change, I know. It takes time. But how much time do we have? How long will you wait—until screaming at the guy who cut you off in traffic does give you a heart attack? Will you wait until the damage is already done and one day you just turn blue and pass out while out to lunch? According to the Centers for Disease Control, in 2015 one in three Americans had diabetes or pre-diabetes, the majority of which is preventable type 2 diabetes. At the same time, most world scientists believe we've already passed the proverbial tipping point on climate change and that it may already be too late to have an impact if we change our ways. Simultaneously, over 1.7 million Americans are projected to be diagnosed with *preventable* diabetes each year. This worsening of personal and global crisis is beginning to spiral out of control; this is the scientific mind's conclusion when faced with these facts. In the mind of the mystic, seeing the interconnectedness of all things, all things are possible and we can reverse both debilitating situations. Isn't it worth trying? Not to some. You've gotten so out of touch with who you are and how much you can control your world to the point that you believe The End is coming for you, so why bother?

The current culture seems to thrive on apocalyptic themes ranging from the religious version to zombies to doomsday survivalist obsessions. The mass media is pushing hard for us to believe the world is out of our control. When we believe that, we don't do anything about it because, why bother? Whether our version of the end to come is being saved in the rapture by Jesus, getting nuked by Russia or North Korea, getting overrun by a giant tidal wave, a fatal pandemic, or plummeting asteroids, our minds have been infiltrated with notions that the end is near and either we're going to be saved (out of our control), miraculously survive (highly unlikely), or we will skillfully survive (even more unlikely) while the rest of humanity is doomed. But somehow, in the end, it doesn't matter what we do because it's all going to come crashing down, but NOT BECAUSE OF ME! We have been told, and now believe as a society, that it's all the other guy's fault. "I do my best. I have to make a living, right?" It's out of our control, or so we've been taught.

When we start to see what we can control in our own personal lives, and make the necessary changes to do so, then we are in control. Because every single choice you or I make influences the whole, as we are all united in the unified field of existence.

Do I buy the easily biodegradable bulk tin of coffee or the individual plastic K-Cup variety? If I can see in the mirror, on the scale, and from how I feel that I need to improve my diet, do I buy the discount white bread bun and processed meat-product from the fast-food place, or do I make an organic salad at home beforehand?

These are not difficult choices when put in perspective of what the real world is and that our own normal, everyday choices are hurting our real, physical world, not to mention our own bodies. Since the FDA has now approved "pink sludge" as meat, fast-food chains have jumped at the opportunity to use this cheaper source of "meat." Did you know that the plastic from one K-Cup of coffee takes about thirty years to decompose? It's estimated that in 2014 alone enough K-Cups were sold that when stacked end to end they would circle the planet more than ten times! These types of daily choices, when made mindfully, are not difficult. These same daily choices can heal us as a whole or hurt us. We really are, as Neale Donald Walsh has put it, "just one choice away" from our glory or our demise as individuals and a species.

Our decision-making is what creates and shapes our world. This can also be seen in the yin and yang of the Tao. Without the choice between yin or yang, if everything were perfect and there were no option to do ourselves harm, then there would be no opportunity to exercise our free will, our power of choice. Without having to choose this or that, we cannot express who we are and who we choose to be. We get to choose our reality on individual, family, community, and global levels through continually choosing yin, yang, or some combination of the two. It is this active choice, this free will, that is the engine driving existence within the ever-changing Tao.

The most difficult part of choosing is opting to leave our comfort zone. Changing to a new way of doing things, a new self-awareness of how our inner space of thoughts affects our outer space of physical reality—this is hard. That's why so few do it without being told to. It's not an easy or comfortable choice. Yet in the end it's all up to you. You control your world with the choices you make. Do you keep choosing things that make you less than your best self? Do you support those who promote fear and stress by paying to see a violent movie or buying violent video games for your children, or do you go for a walk outside with your kids after dinner instead? Do I buy the tiny, little, prepackaged-and-then-repackaged-and-then-repackaged-again-into-a-nesting-doll-of-artificial-colors-and-plastic-like cheese product, or do I just buy a block of actual cheese and cut it myself? These choices do make a difference. Don't buy single-use items whose packages will sit in landfills and oceans for generations to come, if you can avoid it. Simple, but not easy to accomplish, as it requires using conscious choice. Just like self-responsibility, tai chi, and surfing.

These were things I didn't understand so well before living by the ocean so I could surf my fear away. Every day I encounter the waste of the world on my beaches, entirely made of plastic. It's said now that plastic microparticles are being found even within the fish we harvest from the ocean to eat. Plastic lines the shorelines and beaches of every single continent, even the remotest shores at the most northern and southern parts of the world. No land mass is unaffected. There's even a swirling mass of plastic in the ocean, named the Pacific Gyre Garbage

Patch, that's grown to the size of Texas—that's disgustingly enormous! All this filth comes from plastic products we buy and throw away after only using once.

This didn't impact me in a profound way until I touched and saw it firsthand. I remember the first time I saw a sea gull eat a discarded cigarette butt: I almost threw up. I have now seen numerous shorebirds eating various kinds of small plastic debris as well as cigarette butts. The beach is not and should not be an ashtray. I confess that, in my ignorance, I was guilty of this. When I was smoking cigarettes back in the seventies and eighties, I did sometimes throw the butts out the car window when driving. Ignorantly I thought they would degrade quickly and do no harm. It wasn't until much later in life that I learned it takes about ten years for a discarded cigarette butt to decompose. As it does, it leaches tar, nicotine, and a host of other chemicals into its environment. And, as I have witnessed, the discarded cigarette butt does indeed cause harm to wildlife; I've seen them be eaten by numerous birds and carried deep into ghost crab holes. I don't know about you, but if I ate a cigarette butt, I'd get sick. I'm sure a bird would too. As penance, I now pick up every cigarette butt I see. I was part of the problem; now I consciously choose to be the solution.

It's the plastics, though, that are the biggest concern. I've paddled out into the ocean when there was so much plastic trash floating about that with every scoop of my paddling arm, I produced plastic films, wrappers, bags, and such stuck to my arm. The ocean was awash in plastics that looked a lot like the movement and form of jellyfish. Is it any wonder that sea turtles and whales eat it?

It was when I saw a large loggerhead sea turtle washed up on the shore with a plastic bag hanging partially out of its mouth that I never used a plastic grocery-store bag again. The turtle, the Chinese symbol of longevity, had choked to death on a single-use disposable bag. It's good there are recycle bins for these at some grocery stores now. Every now and then I won't have my reusable bags with me when I shop and I just reach in and pull out a few plastic ones to reuse. But I don't know where that bag goes once I've put it in the bin. Do you? That's my trash and your trash, and it could easily escape the bin, truck, container, or recycling facility to work its way into the hungry mouth of a dolphin. With China now refusing to accept the plastic we throw in the recycle bin, it's even more uncertain where these are going to end up in the future. Surely, like me, you've seen many of these bags blowing freely outside with the wind. In some places, these tan or white or blue bags adorn shrubbery as thick as Christmas ornaments on a shopping-mall tree. Our everyday choices do make a difference in the real world that's based in an unseparated, unified field. I can certainly bring my own old, worn shopping bags so the sea life can do without that petroleum-based bag at dinnertime.

All the surfers I personally know are anti-plastics. Because we engage with this problem every board day out in the ocean, we take steps to help solve it simply by reducing our plastic consumption. Mostly it's the packaging of items that's the issue in consumer reduction. It's difficult to purchase things with minimal plastic packaging. I even saw a coconut at the grocery store wrapped in shrink-wrap! Really! Have you ever tried to open a coconut? Nothing will penetrate that shell without extreme force. Does it need plastic wrap to protect it? This was ridiculous to endorse with my dollars, so I went without the coconut that day. I don't want to spend my money endorsing frivolous and long-lasting waste.

At the checkout, when the cashier asked if I'd found everything I needed, I commented that I was disappointed I couldn't get a coconut because it was wrapped in plastic. She said she'd mention it to the produce manager. I didn't really think anything of it, but I did notice there was never another plastic-wrapped coconut for sale in that store. If I am not part of the solution, then I am part of the problem.

The alternative to growing up and making responsible everyday choices like adults is to remain infantile as a species. To continue to believe that always having more will evolve us as a species or an individual or a community is madness. Having more just makes us more comfortable, not better off. We can now easily have a life of convenience in man's so-called real world, knowing that often it will cost our children in the future, and their children too, and species other than ours are already suffering. This is the ultimate narcissism: to believe and act as though my own singular personal needs and the needs of my generation or society outweigh the needs of all. Even children know how to share—until societal norms have gotten hold of them.

This is not a black-and-white question of am I right or wrong. It's a question not of values but of species survival. Looking at the bigger picture of the whole, does it make sense and is it a responsible adult choice to drive a Hummer that gets four miles per gallon, twenty-six miles to and from work every day? The huge amount of carbon monoxide alone that comes out of the tailpipe is deadly. People commit suicide using it. The choice to pollute by driving a Hummer does affect people, especially the cyclists, walkers, and moms with children in hand waiting at the corner breathing that poison-filled exhaust. The choice to drive the metal monster could contribute to the baby in the stroller at the cross walk getting cancer. And that's the physical world. In fact, research from Cornell University estimates that pollution of the air, water, and soil now causes about 40 percent of all deaths in the world. Almost half! The Cornell research and others indicate that environmental degradation and expansive human population growth are the driving cause behind the recent rapid increase in human diseases worldwide.

I know those Hummer drivers don't think they're doing harm because they're not living in the real "every action has an equal and opposite reaction" world. They're living in man's made-up world of outer image and singular, "separate," personal wants. Not fully breathing, not allowing expansion when taking in the world with each inhale.

The very individuals crying out for justice often fail to display wisdom in how they live their own lives. "Don't complain about the traffic when you're in it." If the individuals, you and me, decided to live lives more in line with the survival of our species and we looked at the consequences of every choice we made, many injustices would simply end with no other intervention required.

Since so many believe that survival of the human species is never in doubt, let's evolve our choices from being those of just being able to live on this planet to our own personal values and beliefs. Am I living in accordance with my values? If I view myself as environmentally friendly, do I consistently drive over the speed limit when I know that just going a little slower will reduce my carbon emissions? If I see myself as humane and civil, do I still buy ridiculously low-cost clothes that come from unsafe factories in unregulated countries? If I know my health is not so good, do I still eat out at notoriously bad-for-me fast-food restaurants and rely on the publicly funded government medical system to deal with the consequences? Have you ever heard anyone say, "I'll let my doctor take care of that"? Is this self-responsible? If I start to see that the daily choices I'm making do not line up with my values and the direction I wish to move in, I can take small steps and start moving toward my image of who I am and who I want to be.

Every human being born should be entitled to clean air, clean water, and clean, unspoiled land to grow food and live on. Are my everyday choices affecting those inalienable rights of someone else, either now or in the future? If so, this is not only immoral, it works against the survival of our species; it is self-inflicted genocide. I started small, and one day I simply understood that it was my bad choice to live twenty-six miles from where I work. Eventually, I didn't feel good about driving that far, so I started biking it instead and got super fit and felt great. With time and awareness, I made some bigger and more adult changes, like moving to places where I could live my life from a bicycle.

It's not comfortable, this process of personal growth, not any of it. But it feels good deep down in my soul, like catching the perfect wave. And once I started being more conscious of my choices, I wanted more. I started to feel good about making a difference in my own life instead of just complaining about how things were. Eventually it led me to embracing my values in every aspect of my life and attempting to live simply, with minimal impact, because energy builds once you get it rolling. Energy in motion tends to stay in motion. Look at us: still getting flung farther out through space millennia after the big bang, still rolling on the galactic energy wave. Once in motion, an avalanche is hard if not impossible to stop. It is up to us all, as we are all united in the Sea of Chi, and what one of us does or buys will have an effect somewhere in the unseen, intangible ever-fluctuating field that unites us all as one species and one world. Leonardo da Vinci said, "Learn how to see. Realize that everything connects to everything else."

With a mystic Taoist surfer's mind, I see that our current world problems are all surmountable. When we use our minds, thoughts, and energy together, this alone can and does change the world. I simply imagine and promote and pay for the world I want to live in. I use my energy where I want it to go, not where I don't want it to go. One of the things this means for me personally is that I do not protest on street corners and give my time, thoughts, and energy to the very thing I want to see eradicated. I may inform others about what I know, but I do not feed the thing I don't want with my own energy, like writing that nasty name Monsanto on a sign and waving it in the air, giving it energy. Qigong healing has taught me to be careful about where I send energy in the body. If there are infections or tumors or cancers, more energy can often feed these things. We can see this happen in politics as well. When the energy opposing a candidate is extraordinarily strong and vocal, this sends energy into that candidate, propelling him toward a win even if that's not the majority's choice.

Instead of putting energy into what we don't want, if we come to-gether as the powerful, earth-moving species that we are, we can and will re-establish our balance with the living earth whose energy we not only share but depend upon. Divided as a country, we have fallen far short of the potential of our values. United, we can stand. Could it be that our solutions lie not in new, mechanical, man-made technologies but the quantum technologies of united minds? What would happen if we all joined together in large groups and simply told the planet we love it? Many think this very notion is sheer bunk, but science indicates otherwise. After all, isn't this exactly how the indigenous peoples of all cultures have told us they help keep the planet in balance? They've been telling us the truth all along. As Einstein advises us, "You cannot fix a problem with the same thinking that caused the problem." We are the solution.

Seeing the inadequacies of our modern, scientifically based medical system, more people now than ever are being called to noninvasive, ancient forms of healing, like massage, Reiki, essential oils, meditation, yoga, group prayer or meditation, and many other effective modalities. In so doing, we once again hear the wise words of Lao Tzu guiding us from antiquity: "Stick with the ancient past, move with the present."

Racing and hunting madden the mind.
Precious things can lead one astray.
It is more important to see the simplicity,
To realize one's true nature.
—Lao Tzu, Tao Te Ching

Now, seven years after those first terrifying baby steps into the ocean, the persistence has paid off. I can paddle out past the breaking waves with no one in sight on the beach, and I have little to no fear. I have become comfortable in these now-familiar waters. Instead of fearing the water, I respect its ways. Once I took the time to understand the scary, unknown thing that terrified me, the fear of it slowly ebbed away, with some conscious effort of will. I finally understand these powerful words echoing from various voices throughout our history: "The only thing we have to fear is fear itself." With knowledge and experience come no more mystery, no more fear. The simplicity of this truth makes me smile now. Surfing and tai chi have both led me to believe the ancient masters whose words and lives at times seem so wacky to my Western, yang, left-brained mind.

As a quivering, scared-out-of-my-mind forty-year-old surfer, I learned a great deal about controlling my mind. I had to learn how to suppress my innate fear of being in water, to take my thoughts other than where they wanted to go, which was to "Holy floating suicide! I could DIE out here!" and "BEWARE! There are sharks out here. GET OUT NOW, WHILE YOU CAN!" When I recognized my thoughts were going to the fear (which was nonstop in the beginning), I had to consciously switch that thought to something else like, "Breathe slower, breathe deeper" or "That incoming whitewash is too high to paddle over; I'll have to duck and roll." I controlled my fear and my mind by distraction. Some days that was the entire lesson: just getting out past the break, sitting on the board, watching the waves and other surfers, and trying to control my fear. That was a big day in the (surf)board room for me. Even though there might not have been any actual surfing involved, getting closer to controlling my fear mind was the first step for me in learning the physical act of surfing. I absolutely had to control my irrational thoughts, my mind, to start the process of learning the physical act of surfing. Mind control.

Mind control sounds like a frightening term, conjuring up images of creepy scientists in white lab coats with Coke-bottle glasses in stark rooms conducting illicit experiments using drugs and torture. But mind control is also being able to control one's own thoughts and, hopefully, recognize when others are trying to control them as well. This is an activity with a rich history in tai chi and qigong. In qigong we try to control our thoughts, our internal space. In tai chi we try to control our bodies. The tai chi player uses mind control to be fully focused on all aspects of movement: Are my muscles too tense, or am I using too much force? Is my toe turned in the proper direction to safely make a kick to the corner? Is my center oriented to the correct direction, or am I twisted off course? Is my spine still straight with my head lifted to the heavens? We simply must focus the mind to fully control the slow movements of the body. With over 630 skeletal muscles, this takes great focus and mind control.

It's understood that patting your head and rubbing your tummy at the same time is a difficult physical task even though there is little physical effort in either. So it is with tai chi exercises: consciously coordinating the movements of the hands with the movements of the feet is particularly challenging. This type of mind control is inherent simply in the focused, slow movements of tai chi.

Qigong mind control is often required to maintain focus during extended periods of stillness. For example, a classic qigong meditation technique is called the micro-cosmic orbit meditation. In this motionless meditation, usually done seated or standing, the practitioner focuses on the visual imagery of breathing energy, or chi, up the back center line of the body (the most yang of all meridians or energy channels) and then exhaling energy down the front center line of the body (the most yin of all meridians). The practitioner unites the visual imagery of circulating energy with the physical activity of breathing and attempts to stay focused on this imagery for the duration of the exercise. Some practitioners will engage in this for an hour at a time. This requires extreme mind control, as the longer one stays still, the more the mind wants to wander to other things. In yogic, Buddhist, and Taoist traditions this wandering is often called monkey mind. The mind doesn't want to stay in one place, it wants to jump around like a monkey from limb to limb, or thought to thought. By being able to stay focused on the micro-cosmic orbit imagery, the meditator learns to control the thoughts and use the mind to her benefit instead of being at the whim of its monkey-like shenanigans.

There are also more "mysterious" ways to practice qigong mind control. Those who can master their own minds, it is believed, can then go on to master the minds of others, becoming able to "bend others to their will." Sometimes this is a good thing, as when a qigong master can fully understand the thought process of his student and thus use words and techniques that push the student in a healthy pursuit of balance. Just as you can never have yin without yang, of course mind control can also be nefarious. It is important to understand how the mind can be controlled to understand how to control one's own mind and to recognize when mind control is being exerted over you! And that's happening everywhere!

Yes, even right here and now agents are hard at work in cubicles, offices, labs, and homes trying to produce more ways to control your mind and your thoughts. We are inundated with mind control techniques every single day, and most of us never recognize them as such. What am I talking about? Did you know a lot of restaurants use the colors red and yellow in their advertising because red is known to increase hunger? Think Golden Arches. Do you really believe switching your cell phone provider can give you "ultimate peace of mind"? Or that driving a car will "let you soar above the rest"? These are all attempts at mind control. It's very well done because millions of dollars are spent researching how to control and influence your mind so your money can be controlled by others.

But it's more than television and Internet advertising or the billboards telling me that an insurance company will let me lead the life of my dreams. The mind control being exerted on our daily lives shows up in the very fundamental propaganda of our nation's notion of freedom. We've repeatedly been told in many ways that the United States is the freest nation on earth, yet more of our citizens are incarcerated than in any other country. To put this in perspective, in 2013 the United States' population represented about 4.4 percent of the world's population while housing about 22 percent of the entire world's prisoners. And those numbers keep rising fast. It's estimated that over the last forty years, US incarceration rates have increased by 500 percent! Right now, in 2018, the US is holding 2.3 million people in prisons; that's more people than the entire populations of some countries! According to these staggering statistics, we are not the freest country in the world.

While we Americans are led to believe we have freedom of speech, we certainly do not have freedom over our own individual consciousness. As PTSD and the ravages of war, abuse, and stress-filled modern lifestyle choices become more of a mental health issue, some brave medical professionals are using ancient healing plants to cure our devastating first-world diseases. But for the most part, we are denied the right to experience certain states of consciousness that are induced by healing plants because these altered states do not coincide with a profit-driven yang society. Because it's been shown extremely effective in the treatment of severe PTSD, the Amazonian plant mix ayahuasca has found limited but growing acceptance for treatment use in the United States.

Centuries-old medicines like ayahuasca, the Egyptian blue lotus, cannabis, psilocybin, and others are demonized and illegal despite causing no harm to those who take them or anyone around them. Under the guidance of trained shamans, these medicines are successfully used to treat a huge variety of mental and physical health conditions, sometimes with only one intervention being all that's necessary. Because we are not free to explore these medicines, we are not free to explore our own minds as the most primitive of our ancestors could and did. This war on consciousness is being waged against natural medicines that have worked for centuries and when used properly do not produce dependence, tolerance, or the bad side effects usually associated with pharmaceutical treatment options. We are not yet free to perceive the world as we choose.

We're also led to believe we have religious freedom, yet if my religious beliefs tell me not to do something, like get a vaccination or take a pill, then my freedom of choice can legally be removed from me "for my own good and the good of others" because of my religion. I do not contend that Americans are not privileged; truly we are. And compared to some countries we are better off in certain ways. But to continue to claim we are the freest country in the world simply is not true.

Unfortunately, there are much more subtle and prolific forms of mind control going on all around us. Unless we learn how to control our own minds and get out of our fear breathing, we will always be subjected to the control of others. If we cannot control our own minds, then our minds and thoughts are the feeding trough of every shyster, marketer, salesman, politician, and so-called friend who would try to manipulate us for their own personal profit. Learn to control your mind and you learn how to keep it safe from the manipulation of others. Neglect to control your own mind and you'll spend all of your hard-earned money, energy (chi), and your precious time replacing your perfectly good cell phone with the latest and greatest phone that has one gigabyte more memory. Or the new gadget that will effortlessly give you the perfect body. Or the latest in self-driving automotive technology that will keep you safe from yourself because you can't control yourself enough to keep the cell phone out of your hands when behind the wheel.

To simply take responsibility for one's own thoughts and one's own body seems to barely exist anymore. Somehow, it's become acceptable to sue a grocery store when I slip and fall because I couldn't control even the basics of my own body's movement, like walking. In fact, those few who do exercise self-responsibility and self-control and get along without "accidents" or arguments are not "rewarded" like those who get hurt and sue due to their own lack of self-control. Those who can't control themselves get the reward or special treatment, attention or money. The ones who are causing the problems are frequently being rewarded. In America, there's too much truth in "the squeaky wheel gets the grease." If I complain loudly enough and often enough, I will get what I want. If I simply relax and go with the flow, rarely is my self-responsibility rewarded by society. Yes, we are out of balance here.

There's a remarkably simple principle in education and mind control: reward the behavior you want exhibited. By allowing lawsuits for lack of bodily self-control, by taking up the medical, financial burden of those who knowingly trash their bodies, our society encourages lack of self-control and lack of self-responsibility. By creating legislation that makes it seem as if the government is protecting us (even something like a helmet law), the illusion of protection is created. Under the illusion of protection, we often fall under the magical spell that we are somehow protected by the law and so may slack on self-responsibility. You too have heard someone say, "I'll let my doctor worry about that."

We see a similar thought process all the time now with kids (and unfortunately, adults) wearing bike helmets, which may be mandated by law. Then the kid (or adult) puts earbuds in both ears and plays loud music while biking with helmeted head, feeling fully protected. Yet the law will not protect you from the car you couldn't hear coming around you because of the loud music in your ears. Will the law protect you better than your own ears' ability to hear the oncoming car and your own brain's ability to process the danger and avoid it? No, the law will not protect you once someone has cut the corner quickly right in front of you because they are in a hurry. But if society subtly begins to believe that the state has, and should have, the ultimate control "for our own good," then that is what society will get. Those seeking to control you will in fact control you by regulating how you spend your time and money and how you work, and if this trend continues on its course, they'll control what happens to your body as well. And why not? If you're not interested in controlling your mindbody, you may not recognize when someone else starts to, or even has been controlling you for a long time because the normalcy effect may have set in.

Gratefully, tai chi and surfing have both taught me how to control my mind and how to be mindful. Most surfers don't have to exercise mind control over irrational water fears like I did. Yet all surfers must exercise other forms of mindfulness to engage the wave. When the inexperienced or mindless surfer charges into the water without observing and processing the scene before her, she may suffer. I've done it and I've seen many others do it, even extremely buff, beautiful surfer dudes who look like they live full time at the ocean's shore.

It can happen just as nonchalantly as this: sneak a quick glance to see if there are waves today, then get so excited to have surf after that long flat spell, go running into the water with no further thought only to quickly discover the inside shore pound is incredibly forceful and violent with no way to get past it, like walking into an enormous closing jaw. Yup, I've gotten excited, wet-suited up, and charged out only to get slammed down in the rocks repeatedly in only waist-deep water. I got so messed up once I had to give up for the day after only ten minutes. I got utterly hammered by the ocean within fifteen feet of the shoreline. I never made it past the first few yards because of the forceful pounding of the ocean onto the shallowly hidden rocks. I came out bruised, battered, and completely humbled with dents in my surfboard to boot. This lack of mindfulness, letting my excitement control me instead of controlling my mind, resulted in physical bodily damage, and I had to pay for surfboard repairs.

Surfers also learn mindful control by being objectively observant about the sport. With experience I learned to observe the conditions for several minutes before deciding about going out. How big are those waves really? It can be deceptive when you're up high on the boardwalk. Yes, there are waves, but are they breaking well enough to surf them? Sometimes, even though there's surf, it might not be strong enough to push a 150-pound surfer, or it might just be closing out—where the breaking wave doesn't have a clean, smooth face to surf down, but just a lip crashing down all at once.

Observing which way the current is flowing is important, especially when deciding where to paddle out. If you paddle out right where you want to come back in to shore and there's a strong current pulling to the south, you may have to catch a cab to get back home!

Watching the waves in the sparse boardwalk shade one day, a surfing neighbor named Jeff told me how the current overcame him one day. He had been trying to fight the strong southerly current to stay in his paddle-out spot but got so exhausted in a brief time that he just gave up the fight and let himself drift as he continued to surf. He said the current carried him about two miles south within forty minutes. He was so tired from trying to hold his spot and then surfing that he couldn't even walk back up the beach to where he had parked and originally paddled out. He got someone on the beach to call him a cab to get back to his car! He said he couldn't even lift his board into the taxi, he had to get help, he was so tired from having fought the ocean so furiously. But if the surfer is mindful and uses his head, observing there is a strong current flowing to the south, he'll walk north up the beach before paddling out, letting the current drift him back home, instead of fighting to stay in position.

No other group understands mind/thought control better than those in advertising. Advertising is chock-full of surfing imagery to sell everything from cars and beer to cosmetics and insurance. Why is that when, according to *Surfer* magazine, in 2015 only about .03 percent of the population surfed? Not even 1 percent of the population surfs, but surf imagery is sprinkled throughout all forms of advertising. Why, when it's such a small market? But corporations are sure spending a lot of money exploiting the image of surfing to sell stuff completely unrelated to surfing to people who may live in wave-starved Utah. The advertisers are using the surf image to control what we think about and where we spend our money, which has nothing to do with the act or lifestyle of surfing. Profit is not found in nature, only in the world of Mad Men.

When the general populace sees someone pulling a surfboard off the top of that new sport utility vehicle, then the SUV is more desirable. When the general population sees a surfer wearing Brand X when running to the shoreline, surfboard in hand, then Brand X is desirable because it's associated with the cool act of surfing. Even alcohol comes branded and labeled in surf lingo because we'd rather be seen drinking Big Island Brew than Bob's Brew. Somehow, having things associated with surfing makes people feel cool and good about themselves, and they believe life is somehow better because of it.

A perfect example is flip-flops and board shorts. When I was growing up, I never saw anyone in flip-flops or board shorts other than the tan, strong local surfer boys. Now flops are everywhere: airports, restaurants, ski resorts, even very inappropriate places like basketball courts—dangerous to say the least. Flip-flops and board shorts are now worn even far away from the ocean in mainland environments. I've seen them sported everywhere from Dallas, Texas, to the Appalachian Mountains! Surfing itself has reached places never dreamed possible, with adventurers, daredevils, and extreme sport enthusiasts surfing mountain rivers, ocean-going oil tankers, iceberg-dappled bays, inland lakes, and the occasional artificially generated wave.

In fact, surfing and the image of surfing have become so desirable that it's made some people surf imposters simply to look cool. Now that I was becoming more relaxed in the ocean, I started to expand my vision beyond my immediate vicinity. My awareness was expanding. I noticed a weird phenomenon other surfers had told me about that I had seriously doubted existed: surf imposters. Most of the posers I've seen are white males with good muscle structure. They have the physical makeup of someone who could surf. They walk up and down the beach carrying a short surfboard under one arm, wearing all new board shorts and rash guards, and they never once set foot in the water. When more experienced surfers told me about this, I didn't believe it. But now I've seen it for myself, and it makes me laugh. The poser is using what's obvious and easy to get (clothes and a surfboard) to make himself look like something he is not: a free-flowing energy rider, which is something that cannot be bought.

Lao Tzu tells us, "Profit comes from what is there; usefulness from what is not there." It's the "what is not there," the lifestyle learned and earned by the surfer, that makes it useful in learning about life and useful to society. Now that I was starting to understand the natural balance of cycles in nature, I transferred that information to the non-natural world, the one our species has created. It appears that the Western mind-set of *do do do* has infected most of the world. This lifestyle is typically centered on making money, acquiring more stuff and prestige, and doing as much as possible within a twenty-four-hour cycle—all yang activity designed to produce something. When there is no yin—no rest, no still, no healing or recuperating—there is no balance. We seem to have made alien our unalienable right to the pursuit of happiness. In fact, the Western lifestyle is so out of balance that many people view time off from work as laziness and don't even take their earned vacation time. There are now numerous studies on how this negatively affects not only the worker but the employer, the worker's relationships, and the employee's health.

This overly yang mind-set is what's most rewarded in Western society. It's the office worker who comes in early, stays late, and doesn't take time off who's given the promotion or raise, not the employee who uses his vacation time to relax and enjoy his children. Yang is rewarded and praised; yin is often considered lazy and/or unimportant because it is unproductive. Yet the research indicates it is usually the more balanced worker who takes vacation time who shows up consistently and is more productive overall in terms of hours worked versus output. The balanced worker has rested and so can then give more energy to the project. The balanced worker rarely needs to use a sick day because he takes the necessary time to rest and heal his mindbody. The typically Western yang boss views the balanced worker as average and, frequently, not deserving of a raise or promotion even though he may be consistent, healthy, productive, and works well with others. In the grand scheme of it all, to not have time off from work hurts the company, the employees, and the projects, therefore hurting the community and our world.

Just as yang must have yin, this is slowly starting to change. Google has been praised as being one of the best large companies to work for because of their "innovative" work atmosphere. This so-called new idea Google uses is to let employees set a schedule that is more conducive to their life needs. Allowing the employee to work untraditional hours, take time off for kids, split shifts, and the like—it's following the changing ways of nature. How ironic that something natural is now viewed as new and novel. This shows how out of balance the modern work place has become.

In the same way, the surf lifestyle is in line with nature and the Tao. Just like Google, the experienced surfer has learned to adapt to changing conditions, to work hard when there's energy/chi for surf, to rest when the energy is low. The surfer can't control the surf but can mindfully choose to go with the flow. The lifestyle of many surfers is usually centered not on accumulating things, but on accumulating experiences. Many books and movies have been made about surfers who left their job, sold everything, and traveled the world, flowing wherever the energy of the surf takes them. This is not idealized; it's the way of Tao. To remain in the same easy, unchallenging place all the time is stagnation, not growth. The mindbody is never challenged and can therefore never expand and become more. Yes, it is more comfortable to stay in a cozy apartment where you can control everything. But does actual growth spring from comfort? In the words of *The New York Times* bestselling author Gary Zukov, "Authentic empowerment is not gained by making choices that do not stretch you. When a soul chooses the vertical path, when it chooses to evolve consciously through responsible choice, it becomes capable of liberating itself from its own negativities. It reaches authentic power."

The Western yang lifestyle is centered upon accumulating things to make oneself comfortable. In fact, some of us have become so complacent in our comfort that we won't leave it even if our life depends on it. Think hurricane Katrina or Andrew. Many people died simply because they were unwilling to leave their comfort zone when evacuation orders were sent out. This is the normalcy effect at its most devastating. I don't remember it, but I'm sure learning to walk was not a comfortable, painless process. We fall down a lot, sometimes right on our faces, but still we get up and try again. Thank goodness we didn't give up because it was difficult or uncomfortable. Yet as adults, when something difficult or uncomfortable comes our way, we will often turn away from it, just like surfing or tai chi, because it's "too hard" to do something entirely different from what we're used to. Instead, we remain comfortable and stagnant right where we are. We become complacent and often stop growing as individuals, staying stuck in old thought patterns.

This is where society is now: stuck in an outdated thought pattern.

With a planetary human population of one to ten million people, growth at the expense of nature wasn't detrimental. The ability to continually grow, multiply, and sustain seemed to have no end in sight. With our growing planetary human population of seven to eight billion people, continuing to grow the way we have been is suicide and unsustainable. We are stuck in old thought patterns that are out of balance with our times. To create balance here we cannot simply wait until being told we have to do it.

Let's face it: if governments are tied up with corporations, the push for profit as the driving force of society will remain. So if we're waiting for the government to tell us to stop using so much fossil fuel, it's more than likely not going to happen soon. Self-responsibility for survival of our species mandates that we ourselves take the steps to get off unsustainable systems and live in harmony with our personal values. To know there is imbalance and continue to increase that imbalance is pure insanity. It's up to us as individuals to take responsibility for our own choices and their consequences every single day.

Patiently waiting for the next wave, I sit, I breathe, I think about the balance, the yin and yang, of it all as I float in the ocean's watery equilibrium, observing the natural world around me. I didn't know it when I started out, but now I see that kid in *Point Break* was right: surfing is the source (the Tao), and it'll save your soul if you let it.

Surfing's ability to connect us is so obvious that it had to be noted by a preteen boy in the movie. He could have said surfing is rad or gnarly, or surfing is awesome, or it's hard, don't try it. But he didn't. He said surfing is the source. Now that I know, I must agree. I didn't realize I'd one day take pride in calling myself a surfer and see myself in a whole new light because of it. I just wanted to get rid of that life-sucking fear. It took time. None of it was a quick, easy fix. I had to leave my comfort zone, and often it hurt. But I'm grateful I took those first few painful steps into the unknown and got myself past them.

The waves are slow today, rolling in with big two- to three-minute gaps between the small knee-high sets. I have time to sit here and let my mindbody drift in the field and discover that surfing and tai chi have taught me to be myself in a genuine way, embracing both the beautiful, tan, strong body these outdoor activities have given me as well as my stringy, long hair with sand stuck to my face and sometimes up my nose. Surfing is rarely runway glamorous, despite what the advertising shows.

No one can surf for you. There's no way to cheat. Just because you have the clothes and the latest and greatest surfboard doesn't mean you can ride it. It's not possible to paddle out and pretend to surf for a good photo op for social media. To surf, you must do it yourself, taking all the time needed to cultivate the necessary skills. Same with tai chi. Sure, someone can help you along the way, give you pointers, but in the end, it's up to you to do it, to learn the balance, skill, and coordination to simply control your mindbody. It can't be faked.

While I now have control of my fear, the reality that I sit bobbing up and down in this watery danger zone is still within my perception. I know it's dangerous out here and that I'm on my own. All surfers know that, out in the water, it's up to them to keep themselves alive and unharmed. All surfers also know that regardless of their experience and skill, just like in a Taoist painting, even though they may be immersed in it, the ocean cannot be controlled. So we fend for ourselves, knowing if something bad were to happen, if we were to get hit on the head by our surfboard and pass out facedown in the water, more than likely we would die because it would simply take too long for someone to realize we needed help and they couldn't get to us in time. Lifeguards know this well; time is their enemy. The water offers a lot more resistance than the air when trying to get to someone in trouble. Out here in the living waters of the earth I alone am responsible for my well-being. My skilled friend Mersea can't keep me from falling down the face of a wave if she sees I've taken off paddling for it too late. She can look for me and try to make sure I've survived the fall, but she can't help me. I'm in charge of what happens to me in the water, on the land, and in my life. Self-responsibility.

Tai chi teaches us this in a much subtler way. Thankfully, there's no chance of your getting hurt practicing tai chi unless you're really doing it wrong! In fact, when I've been injured or sick, tai chi and qigong have often been the few things I could do. Even the very next day after the meniscus was removed from my left knee, I was able to do most of my qigong practice. This is a huge advantage over other forms of exercise where an injury might mean not being able to run or work out for a while. In qigong and tai chi, we typically move extremely slowly, minutely aware of every single aspect of the motion: the feel of the ground under our feet, the weight of our arm in the air, the tendons softening in the kicking leg to relax the joints and open them like a string of pearls. Unlike the mindful movement of surfing, with tai chi there is no chance of injury, and it can help us heal more thoroughly and quickly.

Unfortunately, as an extreme sport, many get hurt surfing. In fact, I'd be willing to bet that everyone, every single person who surfs for years, has gotten hurt doing it. I got the only whiplashes in my life not in car accidents but surfing little Florida waves. It's a hard learning curve and certainly not right for everyone. But if you're smart about it and use some sense, only going out when the conditions are gentle, then you can surf into your golden sunsets if you so choose. I've seen many old, gray-haired guys, and some gals too, out in the lineup on longboards on gentle days. It inspires me just like a ninety-plus-year-old tai chi player throwing a swooping chest-high lotus kick and staying perfectly balanced. That's what I aspire to when I grow up. If, like me, you want to live an active, independent graying life, follow Dr. Oz's advice when he says, "Do qigong, do live to a healthy hundred." As for me, I'm not a big-wave surfer and have no need for big muscles to protect me, so I'd rather spend my exercise hours working on functional movement that will serve me all the rest of my days.

Many people ask, "Why does tai chi have to be so slow?" Not only does the slowness build more strength, it is also much easier to have full awareness of the mindbody when moving slowly than when moving fast. You've had this or a similar experience: you drive out of your neighborhood on the same street every day for years. One day, your car's in the shop, so you take your bike instead. You see things on this familiar road you've never even known were there: a vacant lot, a garden gnome in your neighbor's yard, or someone from work whom you didn't realize lived just down the street from you all these years. Slowing down, we see more, we become aware of more. By becoming more aware, our perceptions change. In tai chi exercises we take the time to balance our often-fast-moving lives with some slow-motion therapy, becoming aware of our inner space and how it interacts with our outer space. We learn to move through the world by simply and efficiently turning our attention inward to how we are choosing to move ourselves. Over time our very lives become infused with mindfulness of motion.

Western lifestyle trends direct us to focus our actions, thoughts, awareness, and energy on external space: work, other people, things, our house, inflation rates, cars, church, the environment. In tai chi we explore inner space: how our own bodies move from within, how our breathing affects us, how our awareness, or lack of it, affects us. These are all internal yin focuses; they rarely produce profit so are rarely encouraged in a fully yang, profit-oriented and external-centered society.

When out of balance, learning balance is where we need to start. Shifting the focus is truly up to us. The only profit in it is survival. When we learn how to control our inner space, then we learn a different perception, or view, of our outer space. We start to see how we can and do influence and control many of the moving parts within our field. When there's enough energy pushing the wave, it will break. The choices we make affect the overall waves of energy flowing through and over the earth. As HeartMath Institute and numerous research studies have recorded, human group consciousness affects everything, even down to the very ground we walk on, the vibration of the planet itself.

When enough of us gather into the same wave of energy, it can result in a perfect, heavenly ride or a crashing, destructive tidal wave. Every drop counts. Every person—whether blue, black, white, red, brown, yellow, shiny and new, or wrinkly and old—contributes to and affects the entire Sea of Chi. Every individual choice counts because the energy builds when enough people choose the same thing.

Both the yin and the yang of this are true. When enough people have lost our way in poor choices, the right to control ourselves could be taken away. If enough of us continue to talk, text, eat, compute, and read the newspaper while driving, our driving rights could very well be put under the control of someone or something else, like a robot car. If enough people fail to take care of their own health/body, the "greater good" may have legal recourse to medicate you, and to control your exercise and your diet "for your own good and the good of society."

The opposite is also true. If enough of us simply ride a bike a few miles a week instead of using a car, it has an enormous overall effect on pollutants in our own air and helps our personal health. If enough of us don't buy the too-cheap, Chinese, mass-market imitation-Italian espresso maker, it will cease to exist and so will the factory that pays women on their feet on bare concrete floors twelve dollars for a twelve-hour shift. If enough of us stop using the plastic bags from the grocery store, they'll stop choking sea turtles to death. Every choice makes a difference somewhere in the unified field we all are entangled in together.

Even evaluating the basics of my life—food, clothing, shelter, transportation, sex—and making choices in line with my values, what an enormous impact this has on the world. If I continue to see my sexual habits as beyond my control and randomly create more children to overpopulate the world to consume more food, more fossil fuels, more air, water, and space, then I too continue to be the problem. My perception of myself, my internal space, affects my choices and therefore does affect the future. And if enough people like me (millions) are stuck in old thought patterns, making choices based on habits that are now suicidal to the future of our species, then the destructive tsunami will come because our own energy is pushing it that way.

Every single one of us has the choice to use or not use fossil fuels to at least some degree. If you believe you don't have a choice, your mind is limited. Your thoughts are stuck. Even poor people in Africa have solar lights. I have a simple, portable solar system that powers my electronics, lights, fans, and other small appliances. I'm writing this on my used laptop right now using solar power. It also charges my electric bicycle. Free, nonpolluting resources are available to us all at just a fraction of what you may think. You don't have to be wealthy to make choices for the greater good. Learning to surf has taught me that it's really is up to me what wave I choose to ride. It doesn't matter if the twenty-something, ripped, bronze god of a surfer dude beside me goes for it; I don't have to. So I choose to ride a bike that's powered by my legs and the sun even though it takes more work to simply get to the store because I can, and I know it does make an impact on the whole field. The more of us who ride the wave of self-responsibility, the more powerful it gets, taking us to places we never dreamed possible of reaching when we are divided and separated.

Recently there was a science report on krill in the news that relates to this. Krill are small, shrimp-like creatures that are found throughout the world's oceans. Many larger species, including right whales, humpback whales, and the world's largest creature, the blue whale, all live on these tiny krill. These minute creatures are typically found in enormous schools swimming together usually in the thousands and tens of thousands. In the report, the krill researcher in the lab noticed that a small amount of water was getting pushed by a solitary krill when it moved its legs to swim. A small amount of water was being displaced when the one-centimeter-long krill swam in its tank. The researcher began to wonder about this water displacement, which had nothing to do with what was being studied. He started to do the math of how much water was displaced when tens of thousands of these tiny krill moved together in the same direction. His results surprised him. He kept calculating and got some other scientists involved. In the end, they surmised that the movement of tiny krill together in a school influences the very currents of the ocean!

This is a brand-new theory that would be difficult to test, but it does make sense. If enough tiny krill (or tiny individual humans) move in the same way en masse, it affects how their whole environment works. Humans no doubt have a much more measurable effect on our environment than krill do. We can see the destruction we've caused to our own water sources over the past two hundred years. I started thinking, if krill could have this kind of displacement effect on something as large and powerful as ocean currents, what kind of displacement effect do humans driving together at seventy to ninety miles per hour have on the planet?

I thought about this when I drove Interstate 95 north to visit my family a few towns away. I noticed how even on still, windless days, the trees along the interstate sway and swirl in intense winds generated by the fast-moving traffic going by. It was especially noticeable near overpasses where the traffic wind hits the overpass barrier and blows harshly against the tall pines and palms. If the movement of krill can move the very waters of our oceans, could the high-speed, unified movements of our traffic also be affecting our climate? It makes sense that it would.

The third law of motion states that for every action there is an equal and opposite reaction. This is a concise description of the yin and yang relationship as well as a perfect equation for karma. Karma teaches us responsibility, which goes beyond morality into sheer survival. The third law of motion does not pass judgement; it simply says that if we take part in the cause of something, it's not possible for us to not be a part of the effect. We are responsible for our own thoughts, feelings, and actions, and they will come back to affect us whether we choose to acknowledge this fact or not.

There's no way to know for sure if driving in a fast pack on the interstate causes devastating winds in distant places, fueling destructive wildfires. But I do know that if I'm not part of the solution, then I am the problem. If I can't control how my own body moves through space and the consequences it has on all, then I am out of control and part of the problem, helping to sustain the very problems I complain about. I can't wait for the lifeguard of the government to come and save me out here. I must take responsibility for myself. It's up to me if I survive the wave; it's up to me if I breathe short, shallow breaths of fear, or full, life-expanding breaths; it's up to me if I move my arm with grace or with tense, staccato motion when performing a tai chi move. It's up to me how I use my inner space to relate to my external space. I make the choice. As do you. You have that kind of power in the world. And when we move together in harmony as a species—and that day is coming—then we will move our entire existence into planetary adulthood, acknowledging that we are all interconnected and what I do does affect my neighbor and my planet and therefore the very nature of existence here.

All it takes is a little adult self-responsibility. The current Western perspective of ever-expanding growth will eventually become unsustainable and unrealistic, not in balance with the ways of nature. It's up to each of us to grow into a new way of being that's balanced and in line with our core values. It's time to breathe in a full breath of fresh air.

We're stuck in a shallow breath, a fear-based breath, where "little me can't make a difference with all these enormous problems in the world" is the comfortable, acceptable mantra for lack of self-responsibility. Within a society inundated with fear at every turn, to be in fight-or-flight mode is normal and acceptable; to run from responsibilities becomes acceptable considering even normal, everyday stress. When we breathe fully and learn to control our own bodies, our perspective and our relationship to the whole changes. We recognize that every drop of water in the ocean works together to conduct the energy of the wave, just as every muscle, bone, tendon, and joint work together in our watery bodies to move us. Every part is necessary for the All There Is to be in balance. The poetic Thich Nhat Hhan reminds us that we are a wave within an ocean of waves. Our own rising or falling is interdependent with how the other waves move. When we look deeply enough, we see that our own individual life reaches out and touches everything.

Either we're responsible and make mindful everyday decisions based on the current conditions, the current facts, or we continue to crawl like babies not fully committed to walking yet, not taking responsibility for ourselves. Not until we learn to stand on our own two feet do we learn how to be responsible citizens caring for ourselves and the world instead of trying to dominate it and profit from it at the expense of all mankind.

By changing our fear breath into a healthy breath, we stand united together and inspire the world. A great master once said, "How can you remove the obstacle from your brother's eye while there is a roadblock in your own eye?" We start with ourselves, which at first may seem contrary to "casting off selfishness." But if we are to care for others as we care for ourselves, we must first *actually* care for ourselves. This is not selfish, this is necessary. We simply cannot clear our brother's vision while our own sight is obscured. I was blind to much of the damage I did in the world until the chi arts and surfing washed the scales from my eyes and broadened my extremely limited perspective. It was humbling and humiliating, as the truth often is.

Meet the difficult when it is still easy;
Cross the universe one step at a time.
Because the sage does not try anything too big,
He is able to accomplish big things.
The sage understands that everything is difficult,
And thus, in the end has no difficulties.
—Lao Tzu, Tao Te Ching

To cross the universe one step at a time is just like learning how to surf, walk, or do tai chi. To combat complex problems, focusing on the simple, small building blocks can yield profound results. Trying to combat complex problems with complex solutions can lead to a complex mess, just ask Congress. To keep doing the same thing while expecting different results is insane. We need to use different thinking when seeking solutions than that which led to the problems. To cross the universe on a journey of healing ourselves requires that we start with our basics: breath, posture, food, clothing, shelter, and transportation. These are what I call the Super Six Essentials to being human.

Every human needs these Super Six Essentials, and our choices about getting and using them has a significant impact on our own individual health and well-being, and on the planet's.

So: Are you breathing? Are you aware that you are breathing? Just practicing this several times a day is a perfect place to start. Just by becoming aware of breathing, we change the breath into a healthier, calmer, deeper pattern, which affects our health, our thinking, and our very perception of reality. World-famous philosopher and author Eckert Tolle wrote, "Be aware of your breathing and it will be more powerfully transformative than attending courses. And it's free. Being aware of breathing creates space. It is one way of generating consciousness. Being aware of your breath forces you into the present moment—the key to all inner transformation."

It's easy to lose awareness of breathing when caught up in a busy work/social/family life. This method I used will help you too: tie a small piece of thread or string to your wrist, in a color you like, one you think of when you think of relaxing. Every time you see the thread let it remind you to check in: Am I breathing? Take even just thirty seconds to become fully aware that you are breathing. Notice the quality of the inhale and duration of the exhale. How does it feel in your nostrils, throat, and chest to breathe both in and out? Become aware of breathing for thirty to ninety seconds. Try this simple exercise for one month, and note any changes in yourself that may coincide with this practice. I noticed first that I didn't have so much frustration when maneuvering with traffic while riding my bicycle. I was more patient in traffic, not letting others' driving habits affect my own calm. I was able to "keep my peace" just from noticing if I was breathing or not while stopped at red lights.

If you like the results you see, or if you don't notice any results, continue for a few more months. Eckert Tolle suggests that it may take up to a year to notice life-changing transformation. For me it was much sooner. Just as life progresses, I could breathe, I noticed my body, then I started to become aware of the world outside myself, and finally

I started to crawl. Sticking with this amazingly simple, time-tested pattern of growth can give us guidelines on how to proceed.

Keep it simple. Go with the basics of the free tools we all have: breath and body. We learn to breathe or at least become aware that we are breathing. Then we learn about holding ourselves up, the second of our Super Six Essentials: posture. We must learn how to stand and sit upright in the world. How we hold our bodies relates directly to our health. Just like in tai chi training, when we hold ourselves in natural body alignment—our heads up, shoulders back, tall spine—we have better health. With good posture, we breathe better, our digestion flows, and we have fuller respiration and thus good oxygenation and blood flow to our brain and organs. When we have good posture and simply hold ourselves upright in the world instead of our new normal forward-head posture, we can also see what's around us better; thus, our vision of the world becomes clearer.

In a world increasingly dominated by personal technology, our heads are no longer held up, they are now hanging forward, throwing our spines out of alignment and compressing our lungs and hearts. Our hearts are rarely open, as our shoulders and backs have rounded forward, conditioned to hunching over a keyboard and screen. Simultaneously our health has declined. While our amazing advances in technological medical science are helping save us from our own devices, we continue to create our own problems through simply not being aware of what our bodies are doing. We are both our own problems and our own solutions. Choose to have good posture and you choose to breathe freely, facing the world with your heart open.

A seeming paradox in tai chi is that we often use the word *posture* when referring to body positions that are not stationary but moving. For example, we refer to a well-known sequence of movements as the posture called Single Whip. In life it behooves us to think of our posture this way as well. Not only is it how we position our heads on our spines when still, it's also how we position ourselves when moving through life. Good posture implies using the entire body efficiently from its core. In other words, just because we walk with good spinal alignment doesn't mean it's beneficial to wear down our joints by pounding and stomping our feet on the ground. Healthy posture and movements imply efficiency and ease with mindfulness over every choice of personal bodily motion.

Once we can breathe and hold ourselves upright, we then need to consider the third Super Six Essential: food to fuel a healthy mindbody. Hidden within the everyday choices we make about food are numerous opportunities to have an impact on ourselves and our world. Is this food good for me? Will it heal me and make me grow? Is it available from more local sources? Does it come in polluting or sustainable packaging? How does this food affect me and my world? We start to become aware of the impact our meal choices have and hopefully make more informed, sustainable, and therefore healthy decisions. These healthy decisions will impact our emotional connection to our food and influence how that food affects us, which in turn makes us more aware of our own bodies and their functions.

Is everything working as it should? Can I easily do the things I want to every day, or is something—muscles, digestion, heart, balance—not working so well? Just become aware of the body; try not to judge it. You don't like what you've done to your body up to this point. That's OK. You can make different choices, but don't berate your beautiful life-supporting body by calling it bad or ugly or fat. These judgments don't further the cause of becoming your greatest self, but take us back a step instead. Simply become aware of your body choices and patterns of health or dis-ease. Change what is easiest first, which is usually what we're eating and how we're eating it. Simply chewing our food better results in better digestion and more absorption of nutrients.

As our health improves through better food choices, our vision becomes clearer, our perspectives widen, and our personal choices become more evolved and self-responsible. I start buying an organic, locally grown batch of carrots at the farmer's market instead of the ones the mega store has trucked in from ten states away. I start taking home my restaurant leftovers for lunch the next day instead of letting the server throw that perfectly good food in the trash. This choice alone can save tons of food from going into landfills every single day! An amazing friend of mine takes this a step further; she always has food storage containers in her car in case she goes out to eat and has leftovers. That way, she can use her own reusable containers instead of single-use Styrofoam or whatnot that gets used once and dumped. What an inspiration!

Right now, as I write this, it's estimated that over six hundred children starve to death every hour on our planet. These painful deaths take place while a ton of food gets scraped off restaurant plates into the garbage. In fact, it's estimated that 30–40 percent of our worldwide food supply winds up wasted. And somehow, we still think of ourselves as civilized. Children starving to death while food gets trashed is not the reality of a civilized species. By simply taking our leftovers home, we reduce the amount of food we buy from the store. When we reduce the amount of food we purchase at the store, the store reduces its order from the distributor. This in turn reduces the amount of excess food the grocery store throws in the trash, and yes, this is an enormous amount of food. By reducing the store's waste, more food is freed up at its source. When there's more food that needs to get distributed, laws will change allowing this excess food to be redistributed to where it's needed—school lunch programs or local soup kitchens or even perhaps going directly to those communities where children are dying of starvation.

There's also the impact my taking home leftovers has on the landfills. You've had the experience of driving along and being overwhelmed by the smell of rotting garbage from a roadside landfill. Food waste accounts for up to 40 percent of what's rotting in that steaming pile; half our waste is food! It's not even rotting so well. Core samples of landfills show perfectly intact food items over fifty years old. That apple core isn't rotting in the landfill, it's just sitting there holding on to its life-giving nutrients instead of decomposing and going back into the soil for future generations.

Huge landfills do not allow enough oxygen into the fill for food and other organic material to decompose. The pile just gets bigger with the addition of old cell phones, broken furniture, and unrecycled materials. And with more people on the planet throwing away more food, increasingly huge, stinking piles of garbage will be invading our communities far into the future. Your simple act of taking home your leftovers can help save the planet, especially if you bring your own reusable containers. It will also save you money, overall. That oversized dinner can be used to replace a ten-dollar lunch the next day. Saving the leftovers of just one meal a week can add up to saving $480 on lunches over the course of a year. That's a lot of savings in a doggie bag. Surely we can do these things for our own wallets even if we can't bring ourselves to do it for the future our children will inherit.

While breathing is obviously more important than food, the basic need for food drives us and is an important topic. What we eat makes a difference not only in how our mindbody functions, but also to the health of the planet itself. While there are many facets of food to consider, an often-overlooked but vitally important one is the destructive impact of red meat on the planet.

Many scientists agree with Professor Tim Benton from the University of Leeds, who has stated that the biggest impact people can make on reducing carbon emissions is not abandoning cars but significantly reducing consumption of red meat. According to the World Resources Institute, shifting diets away from beef and lamb could cut per capita greenhouse food emissions in half and slow the growth of deforestation, two of the major contributors to human-induced climate change. Simply cutting down from five red-meat meals a week to two will not only increase the consumer's health but will also significantly increase the planet's overall health. Our choices can create problems or solve them.

Once the first three basics of our Super Six Essentials are met, and I'm aware of breathing, how I hold my body, and what I'm eating, then I start to notice what I put on my body. Are my clothing choices in line with my values? Do you think buying the cheapest item from the department store is helping you or our children? That seven-dollar shirt from China is only cheap because it was made at the expense of others. That cheap shirt was made by someone (usually women or children) probably making about fifty cents an hour for her labor. Would you let your wife or child work in a factory for fifty cents an hour? Would you welcome the fifty-cent-an-hour job (as CEOs boast, "We're giving them jobs!") when your whole day's pay won't even buy one full meal for your family? Once that shirt gets made it's loaded on an ocean freighter that sucks up massive amounts of fossil fuels to get shipped across an entire ocean, then trucked from the port to the distribution center, then trucked to the store, creating more pollutants in the air, just so you can save ten dollars. Do you really believe this is a bargain for your children, overall?

When we choose to buy locally made clothing or even organic, sustainably sourced clothing, our thirty-dollar shirt doesn't add to the impoverished conditions of women and children; it doesn't add to worldwide pollution, and it supports a small business owner who is actually our neighbor, thus bringing more life into our local community so that our own town thrives instead of Amazon. Jeff Bezos has enough money! Share yours with your neighborhood retailers instead.

If we can't quite afford the thirty-dollar locally made or organic shirt, we can "reduce, reuse, and recycle" by choosing a one-dollar shirt from a thrift store, even a thrift store that supports a local charity. Quite a few of my thrift-store clothes are brand-new with the original tags of forty dollars or so still attached because they have never been worn. Yet because it came from the thrift store, that forty-dollar designer shirt only cost me three dollars, brand-spanking-new! This too will have enormous impacts on the local community and the future, especially if enough people do it. If enough energy is moving in the same direction, the wave will eventually break; we'll be perfectly positioned in the lineup as a species to get a long, fun, leisurely ride, and our children will have the opportunity for this fun, leisurely ride as well.

As a self-responsible, aware adult, I start to notice every choice I make, all the while aware of my full, deep breath, keeping my head up and heart open, nourishing myself with healing food from my local environment. Now I need a place to live. There are two housing trends going on simultaneously right now that highlight two ways of thinking: the high-ceilinged mini-mansion and the tiny house. Which one is sustainable? If you think you need that McMansion to be comfortable, I say look at where some of the richest people in the world live. Warren Buffet lives in a modest house with low overhead, embracing the aphorism, "Live simply that others may simply live."

It starts with the basics: food, clothing, transportation, and shelter. The things we all do and need every single day. Are my choices reflecting my values? Am I a part of the problems here or part of the solutions? Are we really a civilized species, as we like to call ourselves, when people live in enormous, energy-greedy houses while thousands of our species dies from poverty-related issues like hunger, thirst, disease, and exposure? Is this civilized? Does it reflect your values? Is a big house more important than the lives of people? More than likely you answered no to these questions.

I honestly believe that 99.9 percent of the human population possesses a "do no harm" value set. I really think everyone here, regardless of country, sex, or race does what they can to help their fellow humans when and how they see they can. Our vision is often skewed by the current conditions in our lives, and we often view the negative cost of doing business as unavoidable; sometimes people get hurt as the price of "putting meat on the table." But it doesn't have to be like this.

To become a species that follows its moral principles we must change how we do business and what we consider truly profitable. The uncivilized conditions that currently exist for millions of our fellow human beings can all be ended if the profit motive that allows and supports these conditions doesn't exist. When we see that by profiting a few individuals at the expense of many humanity is indeed harmed, then these atrocious, uncivilized conditions will end. When we see our neighbor as ourselves, which in scientific fact they are, when we simply see the truth of what is, then we have an obligation to choose love over disdain, contempt, ridicule, belittlement, and hate. Then we will become civilized.

Once aware of where we are and what we've surrounded ourselves with, then we can start to make more evolved decisions; we can learn to crawl, choosing which way to go and how to get there. We move into the last of our Super Six Essentials: transportation. Again, as a self-responsible adult, I ask myself: Do my transportation choices reflect my personal values? Just as it's not recommended for a grom to learn to surf on an overhead-barreling day at Hawaii's famous Banzai Pipeline, it's not recommended for our evolving self to try to change every self-defeating aspect of our lifestyle all at once. It's just too overwhelming, and we don't yet have the skills necessary to pull it off. So be gentle with yourself, especially when it comes to food and transportation. Just do one small, consistent thing to move in the direction your values determine you should go. "Cross the universe one step at a time."

If I see that I'm driving more than I want to or that I'm driving too fast all the time, I make more intelligent, adult-responsible choices. I leave the house a few minutes earlier so I can simply follow the speed limit, feeling less rushed and polluting less in the process. I start riding my bike to work or the store or the post office just once or twice a week. Even by riding a bike twice a week I reduce my carbon emissions and it adds up to ninety-six days in the year I am polluting less. Imagine if everyone did this. By simply driving the speed limit instead of five to ten miles per hour over, I reduce my gas engine's pollutant emissions. I simply notice if the everyday transportation choices I'm making are in alignment with my values and my vision of myself.

Once I can breathe easier, I may decide to make bigger transportation changes. We choose the vehicle we drive based not only on utility and price but also on how it makes us look and feel. It's common knowledge that a car is considered a social status symbol. Because of this, many of us have been convinced that the bigger and more expensive the car, the bigger and more valuable it makes us look. But consider this: one of the most prestigious of vehicles, the Cadillac Escalade, is also one of the least fuel efficient at approximately twelve miles per gallon. Choosing to drive an Escalade says, "I have the luxury of money." Choosing to drive electric or biodiesel says, "I care about the future." Which statement best reflects your values and who you are?

Now, I know not everyone has these options. Many people in rural and suburban America still have no or extraordinarily little access to affordable public transportation and need to keep that old family truck from the eighties running just to get to and from work. I also understand that many people cannot use their bodies well enough to walk or bike and need to drive because of it. For those who simply can't or won't change their transportation habits, consider another food option that has even greater impact: simply reduce the amount of red meat consumed.

Personal awareness of our everyday choices on our most basic necessities like food, clothing, shelter, and transportation is the best place to start. If a choice in any of the Super Six Essentials doesn't seem to make sense other than "because that's how my family has always done it," then I make a more conscious, value-centered, adult-responsible choice instead of being carried along on an outdated family tradition. I breathe in a new life and breathe out the old, stale air that no longer serves me. As we grow into the healthy, balanced individuals we envision ourselves as, our choices will grow with us until eventually we will unknowingly embrace the Frank Sinatra lifestyle with every breath and step we take and every world-changing choice we make.

As a tai chi teacher, I was becoming more mindful of how my word choice impacted my classes. I was thinking about it while getting in a short surf session between classes one day. Here I was, mid-morning on a Wednesday, with glassy, chest-high waves all to myself because everyone was working. I felt extremely blessed and grateful for my life. While not everyone has to work, most of us do, so how we choose to make that money is important as well. I had made a long series of choices over the years to go from making great money with a fantastic schedule at a job I loathed to making a stress-free living helping people to move, breathe, and feel better. It wasn't just overnight that I made the change from spending one third of my life as a jailer to spending about half of my time as a health enabler. What we do to make money takes up a third or more of our lives. We should consider the impact it will have more than how much a mattress we sleep on will impact us. I felt like I was finally working more within my values.

It had taken me well into my forties, but with the wisdom of tai chi and surfing, I was finally learning how to control myself in my daily life that meaningfully impacted my world. Isn't it an innovative idea to try to control ourselves before trying to control what's external? A poorly chosen word in class one day led to a long discussion about what I had intended to say as opposed to what I had said. During my personal sunrise practice ritual the next day, during the *yi jin ching*, I focused on sending all of my energy to my throat and tongue in the third posture. I was living a lie here at my tongue, and I knew it. I realized it was time to let that go too.

How could I control my words well when communicating in my classes when all my life I had been telling little, meaningless white lies? The truth is often simple and for me humbling. The realization of what I had done to myself hit me like a hurricane's storm surge that had been building my whole life. Years ago, I had finally admitted it to myself, yet I had felt powerless to stop it despite having tried. It was an utterly meaningless habit of telling little lies that meant nothing to anyone, except my ego. Usually it was just a slightly twisted truth to make myself seem more credible than I was, or more capable or some other form of self-flattery. Never did it hurt or harm anyone. But they were still lies, and what mattered most was that it bothered me that I did it.

Until this one day. This simple practice of sending all of my energy to my tongue made me realize if I wanted to control its energy, I simply could not lie any more, in any shape. Then I suddenly understood more fully Hamlet's words "To thine own self be true, and it must follow, as the night the day, thou canst not then be false to any man." Even after years of daily *yi jin ching* practice, it still had much more to teach me, and still does. This time, it was easy to stop the nonsense. Only a few times did the notion of exaggerating a tale pop into my mind, and now that I was aware, I could easily dismiss it and let go of my ego's desires for superiority. It's still a process, though, to control myself and my tongue. To convey words effectively so there's no miscommunication is a high art and a skill very few perfect. I'm willing to keep trying, even if it is hard. If I can change lifelong habits and grow into more aware-ness, hopefully I will not be the cause of my own demise.

If tiny krill can change the very currents of the oceans, we humans, the most influential species on the planet, can change ourselves and in the process become the unified, empowered, divine creatures we are—not just in image but also in action. We are our own masters. We cannot blame our fate on the government, China, or Bob from accounting. We cannot blame our ill health on anyone but ourselves. We each create the unified field we all share as one species who will suffer or prosper from our individual and collective choices. We are the solution. No money, no tools required. We already have everything we need. We just must be wise in how we use it.

The ancient masters were subtle, mysterious, profound, responsive;
The depth of their knowledge is unfathomable.
All we can do is describe their appearance.
Watchful, like men crossing a winter stream.
Alert, like men aware of danger.
Courteous like visiting guests.
Yielding, like ice about to melt.
Simple, like uncarved blocks of wood.
Hollow like caves,
Opaque like muddy pools.
—Lao Tzu, Tao Te Ching

Some historians believe Lao Tzu wrote these words around 500 BC. That's over two thousand years ago. These words were used to describe the ancient masters of Tao, kung fu mind, and movement; those masters who had attained elevated levels of meditation and expanded their consciousness and mastered their bodies. Sometimes, in Chinese art depicting these masters, a fire, or light, shines out of their eyes, and sometimes they are empty, hollow pools.

When I first read the above words from the *Tao Te Ching* several years ago at the recommendation of my shifu Grand Master Cook, I immediately thought of my fearless friend Mersea's penetrating lightning-blue eyes, then the eyes of famous surfers like Laird Hamilton and Kelly Slater. In the eyes of these adventurers, these masters of their craft, is the same watchfulness, the same courteousness, the same hollow cave and muddy pool. Then the eyes of my shifu Master Cook also came to mind. I had seen these eyes up close many times during *chi sao*, or Sticky Hands training. His eyes were opaque and possessed a glowing fire and self-knowing confidence that can only be earned, never bought.

Those few whom I have personally met who possess this watchful, aware, unexpectant state are those who dare to push their boundaries and step out of comfort. They are adventurers of both body and consciousness. I have not met anyone who has this bearing of knowing who hasn't earned it. Those who don't possess it have yet to purposely go beyond their comfort zone. They haven't forced their body or consciousness to its limit on purpose. Sometimes the hardships of life create this knowing, and what we might call "a character" is born. This is rarer nowadays in the so-called modern world. With more access to luxury and fewer physical hardships, there is also more sloth and less courage. Now, it seems, only the truly adventurous, those who go outside their comfort zones on the mission of personal growth, will attain the look of the master.

Surfing is outside most folks' comfort zones. For one, it takes place in a constantly changing medium that can kill you in numerous ways—drowning, exhaustion, exposure, hypothermia, or wildlife, including harmful bacteria, sharks, jellyfish, and lionfish—as well as the possibility of suffering a concussion or whiplash. And that's just how the water itself could hurt you. We could also mention the possibility of getting run over by another surfer and having your head sliced open by his surfboard's fins (I saw this happen to my unfortunate friend Mersea); losing an eye to the spear-like point of your shortboard (my neighbor Tim); getting your leash tangled in coral and being held underwater (neighbor Henry); getting your face, arm, leg, or skull bashed in by your board, rocks, a pier, or others; or getting tangled in seaweed (super yucky) or fishing line or net (even more frightening—it happened to me). And don't even get me started on retina degeneration and skin cancer.

Hello, all you young, bare-skinned surfers out there. I'm talking to you! I love you, and just because you don't notice it now doesn't mean you won't notice some skin cancer thirty years from now. Every lifelong surfer I know has some skin cancer. But there are sun-protective rash guards now! If Joe Speedo at the community pool is smart enough to wear one, you should be too. I also sport the silly looking water-repellant, strap-on baseball hat so my face, nose, and lips don't get fried. I look like a total kook, but I don't care. Sunscreens were just banned in Hawaii to help protect the corals that are being damaged by their harsh chemicals. Many popular sunscreens contain chemicals that harm us and our immune systems as well. Don't wait to be told you have to ditch the coral-hurting sunscreen; just get a rash guard and hat—no plastic bottle to toss when it's empty. Easy solution; big, planet-healing effect. Fortunately, as global consciousness continues to rise, there are more eco-friendly solutions to some of these issues. Some companies have started producing sunscreens that are not harmful to humans or the ocean, but they still come in those plastic bottles.

Realistically, from a survival point of view, it makes no sense whatsoever to want to surf. It's dangerous on so many levels that it's no wonder some folks are scared to step foot in the ocean, let alone try surfing. People hazards, water hazards, board hazards, wildlife hazards, sun hazards—if knowing this plethora of unpleasant experiences could be yours if you paddle out, why would you do it? What makes it so darned appealing that the advertising Mad Men use the image of surfing to sell everything to people who will never surf?

This is the very nature of Tao. Appealing yet dangerous. Risky yet inviting. Flowing in stillness. Gathering and letting go. Many outside the tai chi community are astounded to learn that tai chi is a martial art, just like jujitsu, karate, or muay tai. Tai chi is also deceptive; it is not what it appears to be. It is both yin and yang, a soft, flowing exercise that practices sometimes brutal or lethal fighting techniques.

This week, for the first time in my life, someone called me vicious. It was one of my older tai chi students, new to the practice. Talking about the exercises in terms of self-defense application helps to understand how the movement is done and where the flow of energy is directed. I frequently say things in class like, "So you turn lightly and box them in the ears," or "We step up to knee them in the groin." You get the picture.

I was remarkably close, directly in front of this student, showing her how to do a move called the Tiger. I demonstrated the ferocity of spirit that's imbued by the movement while looking right at her, saying, "You claw down their eyes and face with the iron claws of a tiger." She took a step back from me and called me vicious. Later she said it was the intensity in my eyes that startled her. She saw me as vicious, yet it was tai chi that saved me from my violent, self-destructive anger. Tai chi is yin and yang through and through. *Do be do be do.*

While tai chi is a bona fide martial art, I didn't take it up to learn how to kick someone's butt. I started it because I needed to defend myself from myself! The most famous of all martial artists, Bruce Lee, fully embraced this concept. In several interviews he stated that we don't study martial arts to learn how to fight. Instead, we study martial arts to learn about ourselves. In a world that seems obsessed with photo ops and image, an unexamined life is a life lived only on the surface. It lacks depth and meaning. Could this be part of our mental health crisis in America? If we never go within, we only go without.

Now, after eight years of surfing, I feel like I might be leaving the crawling stage of wave riding. I know how to easily paddle out into the lineup, read the incoming and underlying currents, catch the wave, and drop down its face to make the bottom turn. Usually I can stay close to the curl now and flow with the most powerful point in the wave.

I had to learn how to turn in both directions to accomplish staying with the curl. When the ride is over, sometimes I turn out of the wave to smoothly lie back down prone on the board and paddle back out. Sometimes, like a dolphin playing in the waves, I fall off the surfboard at the end of the ride on purpose, just so I can do a little spin in the air as I fall for no other reason than because it's fun. I can finally stand confidently on my own two feet and determine my course even when a small mountain of water is falling around me. With eight years of longboarding behind me now and having ridden numerous kinds of surfboards (thanks to my water-woman friend Mersea), I finally know in which direction I want this ride to take me.

In an amazing parallel in timing, after over twenty years of tai chi, I finally understand where I want to take both it and my surfing. It took me eight years of surfing different shapes and styles of surfboards under different circumstances, with different people, in various places and conditions, to know what does and does not work for me in my quest to conquer my fear and "walk on water."

I've learned that I prefer a cut-out single fin for good stability that's nimble enough to turn when I'm closer to the nose of the board. A thick, fat skeg of a fin doesn't have much ease of maneuverability. It's more like you must throw some weight into making the board turn due to how big the keel is. I've learned that I don't care for the tri fin setup so much, as I'm not as interested in carving out big turns as I am in cruising along with the wave, striving to one day walk to the nose and hang five, or perhaps even hang ten toes over the nose. A single fin gives me more stability in the wave, allowing me to get closer to the nose. The single fin locks the tail section of the board into the body of the wave so I can walk, and one day perch, on the nose, even if only for a moment. The weight of the curling water pressing down on the tail of the surfboard, with the single fin keeping the board stable, balances the heavy surfer on the front of the longboard. It's like walking on a teeter-totter where the fulcrum point of the beam is constantly shifting locations. The hydroengineering that is wave riding makes the mystical me sigh and smile, shaking my head to try to wrap my nonscientific brain around it all.

This knowledge was completely above my head six or seven years ago when these things were being lovingly explained to me as another beautiful surfboard became available for me to try out. You see, my friend Mersea was completely addicted to surfing and would buy and sell boards all the time just to try out different shapes or fin configurations. I was privileged in my early learning stage to get to try an assortment of wave-riding vehicles and have their distinct, individual characteristics espoused to my naive ears. I had yet to learn how to speak surf. I didn't have any idea what the rocker of a surfboard was or how it could affect catching a wave. That knowledge only came from the experience of surfing with different rockers. I had to do it and feel the difference in my body when I paddled out, sat on the board, turned to catch a wave, and actually caught and rode it. Only then did I start to understand surf language: rocker, rail, stringer, side bites, fish, step deck, pintail, floater, peak, trough, gnarly, held down, lip smack, kook, glassy lines, drop in, barreled. This was a whole new language whose vocabulary took years for me to learn.

Now that I could put together some sentences, I understood I wanted to write flowing, poetic novels with the longboard, not a quick, fiery blog on a shortboard. Now I can fine-tune my skills into the nose rider I desire to be, using a well-fitted board during good conditions to try to walk the line and perch precariously on the nose with my arms flung back overhead in triumph. Not carving and slashing through the wave, as is the thrill of shortboard riders, but allowing the galactic chi to hold me up, balanced on a foam pedestal at the pinnacle of the wave's energy, while I rush along in glory knowing this is the present, this is the gift: this stillness of my being while being carried along on the literal peak of cosmic energy. Now that I have learned to crawl, stand, and move, and learned the language of surfing—now I can create the experience I desire instead of being controlled by the wave. Now I can exert some of my free will. Now I will learn to hang ten.

So it is with my tai chi timeline parallel. It is only now, after decades of practice and teaching with only a handful of days missed, that I finally understand some of the complex language of tai chi and can decide where I wish this energy to take me. I know the goal for me is to cultivate my own inner chi by cultivating my outer chi with others and to share my knowledge of the healing arts with anyone who wants to listen. Now that I can proficiently move through a few tai chi and qigong forms and have physically felt the electric flow of group chi go through me, the obvious is clear to me: we are all one. There is no separation of energy between people, between entities, between nations, races, sexes, or religions, nor between us and other species. We are all interconnected waves of energy.

In another surfing and tai chi parallel, just as these activities can unite us to each other and all there is, when our ego creeps in we can also allow these activities to divide us. In surfing we see this in the longboard-versus-shortboard rivalry. In chi arts the same happens with old styles versus more modern styles. While all surfing is the same and creates the same stoked feeling, some shortboarders believe they are superior to longboarders, while some longboard riders don't think highly of their shorter-board brethren. For assorted reasons, ranging from ageism to pride to zealous localism, each may dislike the other based only on the length of his or her surfboard, creating a separation mentality about everything associated with the "inferior" party.

Unfortunately, the same is true in chi arts circles, as ego is still part of human nature. There are many styles of tai chi and qigong, and occasionally separationist mentality can sneak in as slowly as tai chi itself. I once overheard a Chen practitioner claim that modern forms of tai chi aren't tai chi at all. Separationist mentality can lie within a single style as well. I was astounded to experience this firsthand when taking a Yang style class I'd never been to before, even though I have studied Yang style for many years. As the new teacher observed my form, she declared that I was "doing it all wrong because that's not how we do it here." This is the same mentality of fear breath declaring, "Because we've always done it this way," even though it may be hurting us. This is the ego trying to create superiority to be accepted, just like my little white lies used to do for me.

Having studied several distinctive styles of both qigong and tai chi, I've learned that because they are different from each other, distinct styles work better for different things. When I have low energy, I'm sick or injured, I don't engage in fast, *fa jing*-infused movements as found in Chen style. At these times, it's better for me to move more gently, so a very soft, modernized Sun style would be more appropriate.

Styles of tai chi and surfboards are not inferior or superior to each other, but simply different to accomplish different thing. All styles of tai chi work, and so do all surfboards, be they long-, short-, or spongy boogie boards. We must always practice mindfulness so that we don't fall prey to the image of separation and the hate, envy, and jealousy that idea of "otherness" breeds. If we do not continually engage in mindfulness practices, it's easy to become controlled by outside influences and even our own pride.

Having experienced firsthand an intangible connection to what I would call the unified field by going within through qigong meditation, I know that we never have to feel lonely here, as we are never alone. When we understand that all is one, then we can connect consciously to all there is. Once enough of us realize that there is no separation, all injustice will end, all war will end, all socioeconomic imbalances will end. There is no difference between the pure subatomic energy that is me, Lea Williamson, and the subatomic energy that is you, dear reader. We are now, at this moment, quantumly entangled, you and I; we are one, just as the sun and flower are one, just as the honey and the bee are one, and just as you and your blood family are inseparable.

The idea of separation simply is not real; it is False Evidence Appearing Real. Even our science has now proven it. Yet some of us continue in our daily delusion of separation from the homeless guy on the corner, or the cashier at the grocery store, or the dentist whose hands are in our mouth. With iPhones and the Internet, we sometimes lack actual human interaction and can easily begin to feel isolated, lonely, and depressed. We can become trapped by the limits of the physical eyes, by the outside image, the visual delusion. But we all have other senses that help guide us.

My body's senses are often more accurate at deducing a situation than what my eyes and someone's words tell me. Sometimes I can tell that the cell phone store guy is mad as I walk through the door, before I even see him or talk to him; my body has registered the tension in the room. My body will sometimes tell me that the older single man who teaches the class I attend is physically attracted to me. My body tells me this long before I see him or hear him speaking; my body has registered his arousal when he notices me, not when I notice him. The energy moves through the field faster than the speed of light, and some unnamed sense within me receives that vibrational information from the field.

Surely, you've had experiences like these. Walking into a restaurant only to walk right back out because something just didn't feel right. Meeting someone for the first time, yet feeling as if you've known the person forever. Putting on a shirt to go to a meeting and then immediately taking it off because you sense it's just not right. These are all examples of sensing energy vibrations within the unified field we all share. These are not crazy, off-the-wall experiences that we can't relate to in our daily lives. These things happen to us all because we are vibratory, energetic beings connected within the unified field whether we choose to believe so or not.

These are just a few examples of what we can all feel in the chi field that we share. Our current medical understanding of how the brain works is improving rapidly but still has a long way to go. There is still a lot of mystery to delve into; there could indeed be senses that we are still unaware of. Senses that pick up distinct levels of vibratory energy within our unified field that cannot be seen, heard, nor measured. We may all be hardwired to tap into the field when we go within and become still and quiet enough to receive those vibratory transmissions.

The above-mentioned experiences are quite common.

Some of us are just more aware of our shared space and connections than others. When my senses are clean, I am more perceptive to the vibrations flowing through the field we share than when I have allowed myself to become toxic in some way. Typically, I can sense and feel a change in my immediate vibratory field, but not much more. Some more sensitive people can see the energy shifts in the shared "empty" space that connects us. We call these people psychics or seers and typically speak of them in hushed tones as though they have a disease we don't want to catch, when we may want to at least listen to their distinct perspective. Just because we don't understand it doesn't mean it isn't so.

You may be familiar with Allison Dubois, a famous psychic whose work with law enforcement is chronicled in the television series *Medium.* Allison helped various local, state, and federal law enforcement agencies solve numerous crimes over the course of years, some of which had gone into the "cold case" archives. Her ability to tap into the unseen energies of our world helped solved numerous crimes that scientific logic could not. Surely you can admit we humans do not know, see, hear, and understand everything in our world. There is still quite a bit of mystery here. Unfortunately, some see the mystery and dismiss it as hogwash.

To be honest, the evidence that what we don't understand exists is quite prolific, particularly in medicine. Doctors often dismiss as anomalies patient recoveries that don't align with their ideas of what heals. Even when the same so-called anomaly repeats itself, it may be shrugged off as an unusual occurrence with no scientific explanation or even investigation. Miracle cures are documented throughout medicine with the patient attributing it to a change in diet or job or the power of prayer. These are not fully understood by Western science and therefore dismissed despite even overwhelming recurrence of the same evidence. In fact, according to respected CERN scientist Dr. John Hagelin, founder of the Global Union of Scientists for Peace, there is more evidence to support the healing power of prayer than evidence to support that aspirin helps headaches.

To ignore evidence is to purposely bury one's head in the sand hoping it will just go away and we can return to the comfortable world we know that we have control over. But as Lao Tzu has reminded us, "To ignore knowledge is sickness." To ignore knowledge other than your own or evidence is to live in a house of cards built on the insubstantial foundation of "alternative facts."

In a world dominated by science and technology, to acknowledge the unknown, unseen world of energy or spirit is to risk permanent ridicule, despite our American freedom of speech and beliefs. But the evidence of spirit, or unseen energy, is overwhelming on numerous fronts ranging from reincarnation to collective consciousness to ghosts. Doesn't it make sense that as energy beings when our energy leaves us it still exists but is now disembodied? This we know is true from physics, as energy cannot be created nor destroyed. Is it not plausible that disembodied energy could manifest as a ghost? The simplicity of this makes sense.

I admit that it's been difficult to broaden my perspective of what's real, especially with so much mind control going on all around us. But you've had an experience like mine. When my mother was preparing to die, I lived on the other side of the country. My father called me one day, which was unusual, and said simply, his voice cracking, "You need to come home." I jumped on the red-eye to Orlando within five hours and was cruising through the night air berating myself for not having gone to visit in the past year. Suddenly, I felt a chill and smelled my mother so intensely I looked around the plane expecting to see her standing near me. It sounds utterly crazy, I know, but when I looked out the window, I saw a wispy, cloud-like, ghostish form that appeared to be looking at me. An overwhelming sense of my mother saying, "It's OK. I love you. You're going to be fine and so am I," filled my mind. I knew she had passed away. Not a doubt in my mind. I looked at my watch: 12:49 a.m., New Mexico time. I landed a few hours later at

Orlando International Airport where my worn father and brother met me. They didn't say a word, and I greeted them only with, "I know."

Later, even though I already knew the truth, I checked my mother's time of death: 2:47 a.m., Florida time, a two-hour time-zone gap from where I had started.

Enough related stories from real-life, sane people exist that books have been compiled to contain and evidence some of them. Are they true, or are all of us just making this up? I, for one, know what I experienced: the spirit of my mother saying goodbye and moving on.

Whatever *spirit* is, this unseen energy that all peoples on the earth have talked of for centuries, we can connect to it. If we could not, that would mean the entire human population throughout history is utterly mad. All religions are based on the unseen supernatural world, but *spirit* is far outside the confines of any religion. The very idea of *spirit* goes beyond the individual and the collective into a realm we cannot clearly define. To me, it is my spirit energy that can lift me when I'm down, connecting me to some indefinable thing larger than myself. My spirit energy connects me to the spirit energy around me. I cannot see this spirit energy, but I can feel that it is there; and my experiences have taught me that it is real, even if I cannot see it, explain it, or fully understand it. What I have studied and learned has led me to believe that what we call spirit is energy moving in different forms—some large, vast fields like the unified field, some smaller local groups like family energy shared, and the spirit energy that is within everyone. This is all chi, energy, the Force, as George Lucas called it in *Star Wars*.

It is always there, ever present, and everywhere, permeating all there is. It is ever morphing and changing. A relationship with it can be cultivated, even though some are more naturally connected to it. Yin and yang pursuits can use chiForce. It lies both within us and around us. To fully connect with it we must go within ourselves; by going within, we can connect with what is outside ourselves; that same spirit/chiForce energy information travels faster than the speed of light and is able to change and shape the very physical essences of existence, able to share information in the unified field just as fascia permeating the human body shares information instantaneously.

The movements of both surfing and tai chi can propel us into the state of *being*, which connects us to the field, leaving us with a feeling of wholeness and holiness. This spirit connection is so common in chi arts that the uninitiated sometimes think the arts are religious in nature and should be avoided for that reason. For those who have shunned all things spiritual, both the chi arts and surfing can reconnect them to the joy of being part of a larger field, of not being alone, and impart on them a sense of belonging. Surfing and tai chi can reconnect us to the source, whether we believe the intangible spirit exists or not.

This is how they heal us. These natural, fluid movements synch us with the arcing cycles of the natural world to heal us from the damage caused in an unnatural, linear world. We become the flow by how we move in surfing and in tai chi. Because it is utterly and completely natural, we are brought back to a place of wholeness that many interpret as (w)holy. And if you're entire concept of holiness is related to religion, you're missing the connection, simply because that confined, linear, man-made dogma is not what spirit is about. Don't let previous forms of mind control keep you from experiencing all the health and (w)holiness you can. Without the depth of spirit in life, we are reduced to our mere bodily image and life is lived only from the shallow surface, lacking depth and meaning.

It took over twenty years, but tai chi, and now surfing, has taken this stubborn, boxed, and caged mind of mine and pushed it past its comfort zone of limited beliefs. Now I believe what I cannot see and trust what I feel more than what my limited eyes can show me. Our eyes only perceive about .0035 percent of the spectrum of light. We can only see a small portion of our reality. It's not so difficult to believe that in the sheer variety of individuals on the planet some of us might see just a little bit more of reality than others. Anyone who has ever developed a relationship with a cat knows that they see things we humans cannot.

I have gone from "I have to see it to believe it" to "Once I've experienced it, I can't deny its existence even though I may not understand it, touch it, taste it, or reason it." The chi arts have broadened my mind and perspective, teaching me to see into myself, beyond myself, and into the space around me, to look directly at a thing until it shows its true nature. That's when I can see all is one and that I reflect my universe and my universe reflects me.

This notion of the universe and I reflecting each other is not a new one. As above, so below. The ancient Taoists saw this reflection, or self-replicating nature of reality, and put it in the tai chi symbol. Sometimes this yin-yang symbol is shown with the two small dots within the big black and white swoops containing additional tai chi symbols inside of them, then more within those small dots, and so on ad infinitum. This self-reflecting/self-replicating idea is found today in chaos theory. The images of branching and self-replicating fractals are the modern-day scientific understanding of order within chaos: self-replicating order within the seeming chaos of existence. Some fractals have a three-dimensional effect in construction with the deeper, bottom layer looking like a smaller identical version of what lies above. As above, so below. It's all connected. It's our perspective and choice that changes, not the unified field which binds us.

The great Tao flows everywhere, both left and right.
The ten thousand things depend upon it; it holds nothing back.
It fulfills its purpose silently and makes no claim.
It does not show greatness,
And is therefore truly great.
—Lao Tzu, Tao Te Ching

Now, with nine years of ocean experience, I have begun to see that with each session, I learn to flow more with the energy of the moment. My fear is virtually nonexistent as I am present and mindful of the water while in the water. There is nowhere else for my mind to be other than seeing the connection between myself and the passing waves. That is why I come to the ocean—not to sit on the beach or look for seashells or fish, but to surf. Now, all else is else. Tai chi takes me here as well. Now that I have learned a few forms well, I can let go and often find them running me instead of me running the form. In the zone, in the flow—this is where I choose to now be.

Fully immersed in the Sea, I can see the perfect balance of the Tao. Is it coincidence that the ratio of water to dry land found on planet Earth is the same as the ratio of water to "other stuff" in the human body? Is it coincidence that aside from red blood cells, human blood has the same basic components and salinity as seawater? Is it coincidence that seawater has the same density as the human body? I wonder too if it's a coincidence that simultaneously, as we start to understand that elevated levels of acidity in the oceans kill coral reefs, we are also starting to understand that elevated levels of acidity in the human body slowly destroy bones. Is it coincidence that as we see pollutants from the sugar industry contributing to the spread of red tide in the waters of Florida, we also see that refined sugars are poisoning our own physical bodies and generating a diabetes outbreak? Could it be our very bodies reflect the physical world and our physical world reflects our physical bodies?

As physical beings, humans are composed mostly of water. In the womb, humans are about 90 percent water, at birth 80 percent, and as grown adults about 70 percent water. Unfortunately, humans tend to lose water as we age, facilitating the body's deterioration. The earth itself is about 70 percent water—some land too but mostly water. Because of the water correspondence between humans and the earth, we can see ourselves reflected in our oceans. Sometimes our waters are calm, sometimes they are stormy, and sometimes they erupt in a massive wave of energy.

Being now a Taoist surfer and living by the ocean, I began to observe the correlations between my cycles of energy and the ocean's cycles of energy. I first saw it during a category 2 hurricane. I noticed that even though I wasn't stressed out about anything and all was well in my life in every way, I experienced very high-strung, nervous, anxious energy all through the stormy weather. When the ocean calmed down and stopped sloshing, so did my energy. I noted the concurrence of these events and filed it away in my mind with the thought, "I'll wait and see if I feel this way during the next storm." Sure enough, I did. In fact, once I took note, I began to realize that when the ocean was raging with energy, so was I; when the ocean was calm, so was I; when the ocean had a chaotic energy, so did I; when the ocean had a powerful, full-flowing energy, so did I. I kept seeing it to the point that I know I am connected to the ocean.

This correlation I observed in the energy flow between myself and the ocean brought me to the pioneering work of Masaru Emoto and his photographs of frozen water crystals. I am astounded by his work and passion for the subject of water. In the late nineties, Emoto took bottles of tap water, spring water, melted snow, polluted lake water, etc., and had scientific photographs taken of frozen drops of each. He would then expose the water to words like *hate, ugly, mess, beautiful, grateful, love,* and so forth, then photograph the same frozen water droplets after exposure to these vibrations. What he discovered was astounding. When water from any source was exposed to negative words or *even negative thoughts* that water turned into an ugly, misshapen water crystal. When the same water was exposed to positive words or even *positive thoughts*, those same water crystals were astoundingly symmetrical and beautiful. Words and thoughts changed the very shape of the water. Negativity made the water what we'd call ugly, while positive words and thoughts resulted in intricate, refined, beautiful crystals that look like symmetrical snowflakes.

If spoken or written words and thoughts have this effect on water, what effect do our words and thoughts have on us humans, who are mostly water? Is it possible that each time I call my degenerated knee "a total mess" it responds in kind, morphing the water molecules within the knee and keeping it or creating it into a mess? Emoto showed this is exactly what happens with water outside the body. Why would it not be the same for water inside the body? Could it be that our very thoughts and words can harm or heal us? Those who use chants, prayer, or song to do so will attest to that fact that words and intention can, and do, heal as well as harm. Emoto found that water left next to cell phones, personal computers, and microwaves turned into something other than a crystal entirely. The energetic emissions from these devices turned the water into something quite ugly and unrecognizable. Many European countries have taken the research on cell phone and smart meter emissions seriously and have banned cell phones for young people under certain ages due to the damage these devices cause to developing tissues.

One of the most remarkable experiments conducted by Emoto and his team took place in 1999 on the shores of the very polluted Lake Biwa, the "mother lake" of Japan. The lake had become invaded by a colony of non-native Canadian algae causing a very foul smell that grew so bad it was a public concern. In *The True Power of Water*, Emoto emotionally wonders if the stench of the country's mother lake would pollute the amniotic fluid feeding the whole nation.

The lake's dirty water had already been sampled, frozen, and photographed for comparison before 350 people gathered to put healing intent into the lake. The process took about five minutes. Everyone gathered on the edge of the lake and recited the following ten times: "The infinite power of the universe has been crystallized to create a world of great truth and harmony." That's it. When this notoriously polluted water was then sampled one month later, the water crystal photographs showed a much more recognizable crystal structure, not fully symmetrical yet but no longer the ugly blob it had been prior to the healing words.

So noticeable were the effects of this simple act by many minds united that the Kyoto newspaper ran a huge article on how Lake Biwa was no longer emitting the foul odor it had been for years. Also, reports showed that the Canadian algae had stopped growing entirely. There was no other known intervention at the lake other than the Emoto experiment. Is this a coincidence too? Could simply honoring the water change its very structure? Many published scientists, which Emoto was not, have slandered Emoto's work as pseudoscience, yet no one has tried to replicate his studies, and therefore his theories have never been disproven.

Dr. Joan Davis, who studied water for over thirty years at one of the world's leading water research facilities at Zurich Technical University, claims that honoring water is more important than purifying it. In her work, Dr. Davis notes that water responds to very delicate energy and that, when done mindfully, can promote health and healing. When not shown "respect," as Dr. Davis puts it, water is not healthy for consumption for long. She states that what water requires to heal us is not purification but respect.

To a lot of people this sounds like mystical propaganda. Yet these are the words of one of the world's top water researchers. These are the words of the scientist: we must respect water, not merely purify it. The idea of living water that requires respect to heal us isn't just religious metaphor. Science and mysticism, yang and yin. I have seen with my own eyes on many occasions how a human's relationship with, and respect for, water can change how it moves.

As a new surfer who didn't understand the ways of the ocean, it took me several years to notice the effect my good friend Mersea had on the waves. Then, one day, after years of surfing together, it slapped me in the face so hard I couldn't help but notice. We were surfing some small, glassy waves at nearby Pelican Beach Park. It was a cool, refreshing autumn morning. The ocean temperature hadn't dropped yet after the heat of summer, and many people were out in the water enjoying the first little bump of surf swell we'd had in numerous weeks. Even though the surf was super small, several teenage surfers were in the water, hoping, as Mersea and I were, for just one good ride.

As was our custom, we paddled out away from the pack of boys, who were sitting on the best wave spot that day. We didn't care that we wouldn't get as many waves. We just wanted to hang out and chat like adult women while we floated, instead of being inundated with a bunch of boys cranked up on energy drinks. As soon as we paddled out, a nice set of waves came right up to us, and we started our session with some sweet, soft, long, smooth rides on knee-high waves. We each paddled back out after our rides to sit and chat a bit while we waited for more waves. It didn't take long for another unexpected set to come our way. I was grateful.

This time when we paddled back out after the ride, we saw the pack of boys paddling in our direction. They had seen us catch a couple of rides right off the bat and decided the waves must be better where we were, so they were coming to get it. We made our way over to where the boys had originally been sitting and waiting in the lineup. Again, waves came right to us, not to where we had just left. We took a few more rides, and the herd of waveless boys started moving toward us again. With a gleam in her eye, Mersea turned to me and said, "Stay here. I'm going to get rid of these pesky groms." She paddled powerfully and purposefully to the south and out much farther into the ocean. After positioning herself in a place not one wave had broken so far that day, she put out her arms in what looked like a wide, welcoming embrace, and even though I couldn't see her face, I knew she was smiling and laughing a little. I had seen her do this very thing a few times before, but didn't get it until now.

Immediately, the largest set of waves by far came right to her, and she surfed what would be called the wave of the day, which was over-head in height, all the way to shore. Then she paddled right back to where I was sitting, waiting, and watching with my mouth hanging open in wonder at what I had just consciously witnessed. Together we watched as the herd of boys paddled frantically to the spot where Mersea had summoned up the big waves. We sat together in silence for a while. Without words, it became obvious what had taken place, as no waves came to the boys even though they sat there waiting for what must have been over thirty minutes. She smiled at me, her eyes deep and knowing, and said plainly, "I respect the water. We have been friends my whole life. We answer each other's call." And it was true. I witnessed it repeatedly firsthand when we surfed together. I even saw waves get unexpectedly, "coincidently" smaller, making me more com-fortable in big conditions when I was really scared. Truly, I was blessed to learn to surf from someone who flowed so harmoniously with water.

Whether scientist or not, most any person knows that water must be present for life to exist. In the search for signs of life on other planets, it's evidence of water that's scouted out first. Water and life are intimately connected. Is it possible that in failing to respect water, by wasting it and treating it as any commodity that can be bought or sold, that we humans are displaying a lack of respect for life itself? If we were to, as many indigenous cultures teach, honor and respect water, would we simultaneously be reaffirming our respect for life itself? Is it possible that by treating the life-giving waters of the planet with less than sacredness we are devaluing human life as well? Is our relationship to water a reflection not only of our relationship to the earth but to our own species as well? Without water, we die. Without water, there is no life on land. The waters of the earth and our bodily water mirror each other in numerous ways. Is this all coincidence, or do we have more to learn from ancient wisdom?

After that day in the ocean with Mersea conjuring up surf like a water clan shaman, I began to notice how the energy of the various surfers in the water affected the waves. Often, when there was a group of younger male surfers out, the waves would break more forcefully near shore than when a bunch of old guys on longboards were out. The energy of the day's session will often change when someone new paddles out into the lineup. Sometimes the waves will disappear altogether, when before "Jim" came out, the waves were quite consistent. Coincidence? I noticed that usually when dolphins were around, riding waves along the coastline, the energy in the water was more playful. I've been out to surf near surf competitions, and I can tell you, the energy in the water was not playful when most everyone in the water was trying hard to outdo each other and win instead of just enjoying the surf. One time this competitive energy was so intense, I felt like I was swimming in testosterone even though I was about a block away from where the competition was taking place. Truly we are all connected in the Sea of Chi. Our thoughts, our energy, our very vibrations of intention, affect the water-like fields surrounding us.

Becoming more aware of water, I realize what I read in the *Tao Te Ching*. Water does not discriminate. It treats all people the same—whether strong or not, whether young or not. Water doesn't care what you drive, wear, or have in the bank. Water levels us to equal ground. We must all drink it or die. When we're in it, we do well to go with the flow and not resist it. Because it is in us all, we all can move with the flowing grace of water. Water never loses balance, as it always seeks level ground. Water is rarely hampered by obstacles; it flows around them, eventually wearing down that which wishes to contain it. Water moves both fast and slow; when stagnant it breeds decay.

Since we are all made mostly of water, many of its attributes can be found within us. Flowing in harmony with your world is your basic physical nature. Treating all people as equals, attempting not to rise above but to find level ground together as one. In seeing ourselves as the water we are, we learn to flow together. This is the lesson embodied in both surfing and tai chi: be who you are from your centered core of being, flowing in harmony with the wave you choose to ride.

Water, as the great equalizer among humans, is, similarly, the great humbler. We are all the same basic flesh and bone and water, none of us greater or lesser in our physical essence. We are all drawn to it, the water that unites us, be it the ocean, river, stream, or lake. The water calls us back to itself, like a magnetic force trying to reunite all of its separate parts. One day, in this new Age of Aquarius, water will unite us and heal us from our metal-dominated world of steel, copper, and gold. As water smooths away the sharp edges of all metals, may it smooth away our differences so we may flow as one in our Sea of Chi.

The ancient Taoists were indeed scientists, as they were the first to use scientific formulations and in fact invented anesthesia. It is the shared empirical scientific act of objective observation that has finally led physicists to draw the same conclusions as these ancient Taoist scientists: all is one in the Sea of Chi. Or in more science-y terms: there is no separation within the unified field. Both statements refer to the same thing. Quantum physics has validated several ancient Taoist understandings; the unified field/Sea of Chi idea is but one of these ideas. The ancient masters of mindbody have left us a treasure trove of self-healing biotechnology based on the high science of objectively observing the natural world. They devoted their entire lives to these pursuits without distractions like computer games, car shopping, window tinting, or sitcoms. All of their time was devoted to their high science; the ancient chi arts they have left us are a testament to their extreme powers of observation and understanding of Tao.

The Taoist refers to the Sea of Chi and points out that all chi occupies the same space and since there are no boundaries to chi, it all merges into itself on various levels. The quantum theorists say the same thing: within the unified field, all fundamental forces and elementary particles exist within the same field so are not separate. The surfer gets this right away: many waves make up the ocean, none of them separate. It is because of this unified field that what happens to one wave ripples out and affects the adjacent wave, the whole ocean, and the whole connected field. When the water is very calm, just one tiny foreign particle falling on the surface sends energy obviously rippling out infinitely. What fell as one drop within the vast sea influenced the entire sea, the whole field. Nothing is separate here.

The scientist has yet to prove the unified field, but the theory exists in many specialties: gravity, electromagnetism, radiation, hydrodynamics, particle physics, music theory, early childhood education, system theory, surfing, Christianity, and the many components of Taoism, tai chi being one example.

I'm sure you yourself have experienced some tangible relationship to the All Is One. Have you ever walked into a room and known right away an argument was taking place? Just felt the tension in the air? Have you ever been thinking about someone right before she called?

Has something horrible ever happened to a family member and at the same time you just knew something was wrong only to find out later you were right? Have you ever taught someone something that you yourself were taught and then felt a sense of completion in this passing on of knowledge and skill? Have you ever had a sinking feeling in your gut only to find out unwelcome news had befallen a loved one? Have you ever just known you would get the job or the date or the house the moment you saw it? Have you ever been able to tell, without a word being spoken, when it's best to leave someone alone rather than engage him? Have you ever walked into a church, temple, or sacred space and felt goose bumps and a sense of overwhelming awe and peace?

I could go on and on, but you get the idea. You've had one if not more of these experiences. Experiences you couldn't quite explain with your logical mind but that you simply knew through and through were true. Just like scientists, knowing the unified field exists but somehow not able to pin it down, to dissect it in full, to "prove" it's what most would accept as real. As Lao Tzu told us at the beginning of this journey, "The Tao that can be told is not the eternal Tao."

But when it's truth, you usually know it. Universal truths are accepted by all, regardless of language and our ability, or inability, to describe that truth. All over the world we know it's unacceptable to harm another person. That doesn't mean we've stopped harming each other, just that we mostly all agree that we shouldn't. It's a given truth of our species. We know we should foster our children into good and meaningful lives; we don't always do it, but all cultures know this to be true. Same with the unified field/Sea of Chi. We all experience it to be true, even though we can't explain it and certainly don't often act on it as truth.

This could be part of why surfing and the surf lifestyle are considered so cool and desirable that millions of advertising dollars are spent portraying the surfer's fluid flight to people who may only see the ocean once in their lives while on vacation. Surfing visually shows us the truth and beauty of man with nature. With the graceful art of surfing, the harmonic interaction of natural balance possible between humans and nature is right in your face. It's obvious. When we see someone surf a wave well, we as spectators are drawn into this balance. Watching a surfer flow, we too flow with that grace and seeming effortlessness, even if just for an instant, as the mere act of observation makes us quantumly entangled. Innately, we understand on viewing the surfer that a delicate balance has been achieved, one that is natural, wholesome, and beautiful.

This underlying connection with the ways of nature helps make surfing and the surf lifestyle so appealing. The lifestyle of the surfer is not confined to yang, boxed, categorized, separationist thoughts or actions. The surfer is seen as absolutely free, outside the nine-to-five cubicle drudgery that many endure. This is the appeal: the way of nature, the real world versus the man-made world that confines us in straight, unnatural, man-made lanes, grids, and boxes. The surfer arcs and flows, living outside the boxes to which most people confine themselves, creating a life of effortless effort that is connected to the natural, real world.

Surfers often become environmental activists as they become more aware of how disposable plastics and other pollutants affect the oceans, and they usually live by the ocean so they can stay close to surf without driving far. Some surfers travel a lot in search of good waves, making them not so carbon emission friendly. This is especially true of professional surfers who make money traveling the world and surfing in competitions. However, it's been my experience that most surfers stick close to their local surf spots, their favorite breaks, and only occasionally travel, if ever, for surf. I have never flown anywhere for the sole purpose of surfing. I have the whole central east coast of Florida to hunt down waves on; that is enough. Many consider coastal Florida a tropical paradise, so why would I get caught up in "the grass is greener on the other side" mentality when I can appreciate what I have right where I live? This, too, I have learned from tai chi and surfing: accept what I have and be profoundly grateful for it, live in it, savor and cherish the present, being fully aware of and grateful for it all.

Because the local surfer knows she can't rely completely on the not so accurate surf forecasts, she typically stays close to home in case the surf picks up. She shops close to home, works close to home, and tends to be relaxed and happy not dealing with as much traffic. This has a significant impact on her whole field along with everyone she encounters, and the choices she makes tend to become eco-friendlier due to her very real immersion in the earth itself. Mindful surfers are typically environmentalists in that they see the relationship of each of us to the earth.

The mindful surfer is aware of the toxic water conditions after it rains. If the beach is one that's close to an urban area, every rain floods the local surf break with street runoff that includes all manner of foul things. Every pesticide, herbicide, and fertilizer used on the local lawns, including the dreaded cancer-causing Roundup, eventually makes its way to the ocean. Would you swim in Roundup? Would you want children swimming in Roundup? The mindful surfer starts to see how his individual choices affect the planet and starts to live more simply, closer to the earth, in a more sustainable way, simply because he doesn't want to poison himself; it's self-responsibility. Many surfers suffer from strange water-borne illnesses that the MD somehow can't quite figure out what it is or how to stop it. I've known surfers who were plagued for years because of what's flowing into our planet's life-giving water.

One person's decision to learn to surf affects the entire field. Now, I'm not saying everyone should move to the coasts and learn to surf. That would obviously lead to mayhem. What I am saying is that the mindful surfer, through her art, slowly learns about the unified field and how her choices affect that field. If she is mature enough, once she recognizes this, she will change some of her decision-making to healthier picks. If she is not, she will live a life that's not true, not in line with her values. A life where even though she sees the unity of all, she acts as though she's separate and that what she does or buys doesn't matter to the whole. This is an immature choice, for to deny the truth, in the end, simply doesn't work. As Lao Tzu put it, "To ignore knowledge is sickness." To live knowingly within a lie, not acting in accord with one's beliefs, is a source of madness and discord, being out of harmony with one's self.

Having now experienced how two different moving exercises have transformed my very perception of reality, my emotional awareness, and my physical health, I'm beginning to respect the mindbody connection. Truly, there is no difference between the mind and body, as science has already proven. I have used my body to overcome my mind. I somehow found myself in a place where the physical activities of both surfing and tai chi have healed my mind, my emotions, and my spirit. They have taught me to live in harmony with myself and my core values.

This is part of the allure of surfing: the surfing lifestyle can heal us and bring us back to balance by establishing a relaxed, go-with-the-flow, natural lifestyle. Most depictions of surfers in mass media, outside of advertising, are not so flattering or realistic. In the film industry, surfers are generally depicted as slackers, drug users, young, not so intelligent, criminals, or typically low down on the social scale. I'm reminded of Jeff Spicole in *Fast Times at Ridgemont High*, the gang of bank-robbing surfers in *Point Break*, and the newest surfing criminals in the premier channel series *Animal Kingdom*.

If the media were to accurately depict those who surf, they would be strong, healthy, dedicated athletes who've been able to carve out their own place in the world despite having to go against the norm to get there. Surfing is often seen as a slacker activity and sometimes discouraged by parents or family who simply don't understand it. A 2011 Surfrider Foundation survey found the average surfer is thirty-four years old, makes $75,000 per year, and spends about two and a half hours in the ocean during each surf session. That doesn't sound at all like a drug-hazed slacker. To surf for two and a half hours, or to simply be in the ocean for that long, takes the physical stamina of an athlete. Earning a reported $75,000 a year average income certainly isn't the result of not trying.

In truth, surfers are some of the healthiest people, in both mind and body, that I've ever met. They look healthy, they exude a playful joy in the world, and they know how to relax and let go of the hectic stress of the man-made world. It's the relaxed, healthy, natural lifestyle that makes surfing so appealing. We innately realize that this can help us feel better in our own lives. And truly it can. It certainly did for me. This same relaxed, healing lifestyle is also attainable through the ancient healing arts of tai chi and qigong. Both have taught me a better way to live that's more in balance with my own personal values simply by consistently practicing my forms. Here I repeat the hopeful words of Eckert Tolle, "Spiritual practices that involve the physical body, such as tai chi, qigong, and yoga, are also increasingly being embraced by the Western world. These practices . . . are helpful in weakening the pain-body. They will play a significant role in the global awakening."

It wasn't until I read these words in *A New Earth* that I realized why, when approaching fifty years old, I have no pain in my body. The medical research supports the testimony that practicing tai chi and qigong helps to alleviate various forms of physical pain. I have lived most of my life pursuing what might be considered extreme sports for fun and personal growth: running one of the world's most difficult marathons, the Bataan Memorial Death March, twice; doing off-the-ground mountain-biking jumps with no helmet or protective gear whatsoever—and falling a lot; surfing; skydiving; caving; sandboarding; rock climbing; and skateboarding. I have sustained quite a few injuries for which I never consulted a doctor, and still, I have little to no pain on a regular daily basis in my well-used Generation X body. It wasn't until I read the above words from Tolle that I realized tai chi had healed my pain body, on many levels, and these ancient biotechnologies can do the same for anyone.

Studies attest to the capacity of the chi arts to help alleviate both acute and chronic pain. According to Dr. Peter Wayne in *The Harvard Medical School Guide to Tai Chi*, the mechanisms of how tai chi helps with pain include both physical and psychosocial awareness. The physical aspects of pain relief from tai chi relate to our posture and skeletal alignment, attention to the waist and hips, alignment of feet, staying relaxed, awareness of breath, and using only 70 percent of our full range of motion. It's been shown that traditional tai chi exercises use about 90 percent of the possible movements of the human body, thus safely and effectively maintaining the body's full range of motion without straining it, helping to alleviate common joint pains. The breathing aspect of tai chi pain relief is also part of the meditative and psychological healing that takes place. Dr. Wayne goes on to state that he believes the social interaction found in tai chi classes also contributes to the lessening of pain perception, but that more studies need to be conducted here.

At a time when the news is filled with the devastations caused by an opioid crisis in America, it seems obvious that a cost-effective and proven treatment protocol that involves tai chi and qigong is sustainable, effective, and economical. And why not? It doesn't cost much, puts the power of the healing process in the practitioner's hands (not the doctor's or insurance company's), it works, is nonaddictive, has no bad side effects, and enhances other aspects of mindbody health besides pain. It's a win-win all around. Tai chi and qigong can heal us on multiple levels if we simply do these practices that are calming and enjoyable. The very act of engaging in these exercises creates a centered, healing effect that ripples out from our core into the field we all share, thus helping to shape a healthier community and world.

It's this alert yet relaxed way of being that shapes the lifestyle of the Taoist. This is some of the underlying appeal of both tai chi and surfing, and how both create a better world. The surfer and the tai chi player both know how to let go and flow in profoundly similar ways. As anyone who's tried it will tell you, it takes years to really learn to surf, just as it takes years to cultivate the mindbody art of tai chi chuan. The relaxed, laid-back, go-with-the-flow lifestyle that's created in individuals through years of training in either tai chi or surfing, can shape the person, the family, and the community they are in, and, ultimately, the world in a way that brings us all back into balance. This, to me, is the realm of the unknowable about the similar surfing and chi lifestyles: how this nonprofit, unstructured way of living affects the ebb and flow of energy on the whole planet. Practicing both surfing and tai chi produces nothing tangible but produces healing results. As Lao Tzu told us long ago, "Profit comes from what is there. Usefulness comes from what is not there."

We know that certain lifestyles contribute to and cause certain dis-eases, and that the proliferation of these lifestyles and thus these dis-eases affects not only the individual experiencing it but also her family, her community, and the world. The very lifestyle of the individual affects the whole because our world is a sum of its parts; if enough of its parts are doing something stressful and destructive, "racing and hunting" as Lao Tzu put it, then our world will be stressful and destructive. Just as we see our society fracturing apart and becoming separationist in many actions and beliefs, at the same time we witness the health of our individual citizens deteriorating en masse. What we see in our culture and mass media tends to have an enormous influence on our personal and societal lives. What are you allowing yourself to see? Are you inviting in images and energy of violence and destruction? What are you paying to promote? How does your life and lifestyle affect your family, your community, your earth? Is your very lifestyle poisoning you and the future of your progeny's planet?

We know from years of scientific research on the brain that it cannot distinguish between what is real and what is not real simply from the visual stimulation it receives. When our eyes see something violent or stressful, our entire physical organism responds as though it is going into a fight-or-flight situation, whether that visual information is coming from something happening right in front of us or a video game or even the nightly news. If you are someone who consistently wakes up and goes to bed with the world or local news, you are kicking in your body's stress hormones, either at the end of your day when your body needs to relax, rest, and heal, or at the very start of your day. Both scenarios are slowly and consistently generating mindbody stress whether you choose to acknowledge it or not. Be kind to yourself. Simply by choosing not to expose yourself to stress at these crucial times of the day, you are creating better overall health and well-being. The journey to health is not only about food and exercise.

In the yin and yang of it all, it makes sense that an overly yang *do* lifestyle can balance by practicing nonproducing, *being* mindbody practices. This can help restore balance. Because of this, I see the Taoist surf and Frank Sinatra lifestyles being necessary for balance to the whole. I think this is what renowned consciousness explorer Dr. Timothy Leary saw when he said, "Surfing is the ultimate lifestyle." He understood that the lifestyle learned and demanded by becoming a dedicated surfer affects the individual in a healthy way that keeps her family healthy, that doesn't drain her community and therefore contributes to actual progress in her community instead of always fighting dis-ease. You could say that when we are at ease, dis-ease cannot exist.

Over the last eight or nine years of living on this barrier island, this has become clear to me as I observe the yin-and-yang flow of it all. Everyone who lives in this area knows exactly what I'm talking about. The vibe here is relaxed, calm, peaceful, and astonishingly crime-free. People let their kids roam all over, unsupervised. The people who live on this tiny, little, vulnerable strip of sandbar don't like to drive two miles over the causeway to get to the mainland. The mainland's vibe is different, more like a city's, which Melbourne, Florida, now is. It's fast, bumper-to-bumper driving, sometimes on tiny roads that were not designed for the volume of traffic they convey. There's honking, the air stinks, people are tense, yet it's just two miles away from the relaxed beach life. Some may think this observation is just because I live on the beach and the beach is always more relaxed. This is not the case. If you've ever been to Miami Beach, Ft. Lauderdale Beach, Sarasota's beaches, or many other beachside communities in Florida, you know they are not relaxed. It's not the beach itself that creates the vibe of the community.

There's certainly no denying that the relaxed surf-lifestyle vibe pervades this whole island, as people who live out here are likely to enjoy copious amounts of time with the ocean and there's a disproportionate number of surfers compared to just over the bridge. The lifestyle of the general population has affected the health and overall well-being of everyone who chooses to live here. Even temporary tourists notice it, not just those of us who live in the area full time. The beach side is relaxed and has a desirable lifestyle; just over the bridge does not. Everyone becomes aware of this shift in the energetic field that occurs just by crossing a bridge.

Having lived a Tao surfing lifestyle now, I can finally understand that the depth of the experience cannot be fully described, it cannot be told, just as the Tao cannot be told. We can talk about it and we can experience it, but these two do not carry the same understanding. To understand surfing, you must do it. "Only a surfer knows." To understand the Tao, you must live it, not just read about it. To live the Tao, you must use your mind to see the natural balance of things and correct imbalances when they arise.

To live like a surfer is to be in the moment, not just in the water, when performing one's art. To surf, one must be on call for the ocean, especially in a place with inconsistent surf like Florida. To surf here is, by necessity, to learn how to go with the flow of the ocean and not your own personal desires. There have been times when I didn't feel like going out when the surf was perfect, but this could be my only opportunity all flat-summer long, so I kind of half-heartedly pulled out a longboard and slowly and unenthusiastically waded into the ocean only to discover that the ocean knows how things flow better than I do. Once immersed in the living waters of the earth, I start feeling better and better. My mind becomes clearer, my energy increases, and my enthusiasm returns; my spirit is lifted. Surfing has healed me, but it's not necessarily done when and how I prefer. So it is to learn how to flow, to learn how to let go of our tight grip, to learn how to adapt to changing conditions.

Fortunately, to play tai chi and qigong is much more convenient than surfing and can easily fit in any lifestyle anywhere. Only about twenty minutes a day can have profound healing effects that ripple out in a cosmic wave of energy. This is the beauty of even the simple, profound practice of Stand, Relax, Breathe. It can be done by anyone, anywhere, anytime, making it the most readily available form of healing on the planet. Universal truths apply to all, not just the rich or the educated. This is the healing power of chi. It is always there for anyone to tap into, no special club, clothes, board, conditions, or the like needed. Just engage and the healing begins.

Unlike a doctor, the chi arts do make a promise of health after treatment. No Western-trained medical doctor will claim that "you will definitely feel better and notice improvement from this treatment." There is no guarantee all of your time, money, and energy spent on a Western medical treatment will help you. Remarkably, this is not the case with the chi arts. As Roger Jahnke, DOM, so aptly put it, "This is the healing promise of chi: if you do it, you will feel better." This promise has upheld itself to me.

The tai chi and surf lifestyle is also one that's intimately connected to the natural flows of energy, whether they take place in our environment or our relationships. To go with the flow means to observe the energy of the situation—whether it's an incoming wave, current ocean conditions, how mad your wife or boss is, or the direction of a punch that's coming at you—to read the energy of the situation, choose to let it roll past us or engage it, and perhaps follow that energy gracefully until it's gone, with no harm in the process. This is to understand the flow of energy in nature, the natural cycles that rise and fall, the ever-changing yin and yang of it all. To go with the flow is not the lifestyle of the modern age. Rather, Western lifestyle focuses on being in control of the situation, dominating the energy of the moment, and trying to use it for personal profit.

The entire life of the tai chi master and dedicated surfer is like water flowing effortlessly through its natural course: sometimes fast—you're dropping down the face of a building barrel, or warrior breathing to generate energy; sometimes slow when conditions are small or flat, or in the stillness of standing meditation. The Western lifestyle has no cycle of on/off, high tide/low tide, yang or yin. The Western lifestyle is always on, always yang, always go, always do. In fact, those who are the most out of balance become the most financially rewarded, thereby perpetuating the imbalance.

This is a world with only the fiery heat of summer, never getting a winter to cool off. This is a lifestyle that modern medical science now understands is very unhealthy, yet a lifestyle that the modern medical industry itself perpetuates by having interns and doctors work grueling hours with little to no time for rest, making them more prone to mistakes. This lifestyle causes stress that contributes to and often is the very cause of heart attacks, hypertension, autoimmune problems, and a host of other Western lifestyle diseases.

By knowing how to let go and relax, the surfer and the tai chi practitioner contribute to their overall health and the overall health of society, helping to create balance. I hope that deep down this is part of the surfing allure, the innate desire of humans to want to help their world to flourish by being more relaxed and less stressed. I think this may be why I've had several people tell me, "I like the image and idea of tai chi." The image of both the tai chi player and the surfer is relaxed and balanced, contributing to their mass appeal.

What one gains by physically surfing waves (not surfing the web) or studying the Tao through tai chi is true knowledge. What one gains through web surfing is information, much of it false and terroristic in nature. It's terroristic in nature because a great deal of it is meant to scare, intimidate, control, misinform, or even bully coach—all of which are terrorist acts. The only terroristic thing about really surfing is the imagery of shark attacks perpetuated by the popular media. Information is tangible; it can be written down, sold, recorded, and manipulated; it is very yang and hard in nature. Knowledge can be perceived as more yin because it is exceedingly difficult to write down what you know and convey the true meaning with the feeling and depth of that knowledge. Knowledge is more difficult to attain, as it cannot be bought or sold, only gained through observation and experimentation with the information given. Whereas, information is bought and sold daily.

Learning to become centered by balancing yang with yin is both a physical and metaphorical act and can be achieved by practicing tai chi and qigong. Hopefully, I've shown it can also be achieved by learning to surf waves. Both physical activities seek the same thing: to move and flow like water, and the similarities just start there. In both activities the practitioner must have a particularly good understanding of her center of gravity and keep her balance through a myriad of changing positions. The common bow stance of tai chi and the surfboard stance are the same, as are how the body is moved from its core; moving from our center, using the center of gravity (where the lower *dan tien*, or energy center, is located) to propel our energy forward or to mindfully withdraw it.

Now that I've progressed a bit in both tai chi and surfing, I can see that the silk-reeling style of movements (found in Chen and other tai chi forms) mimics the energy of a wave. The energy spirals out from its core and unleashes in a whipping force that can make a small movement knock a man off his feet, or power a tiny ocean curl with enough energy to propel a 180-pound surfer. The power in these movements comes not from how big they are, but in how the spiral unwinds its energy, just like a wave. The ancient knowledge wound up within the chi form unwinds my mindbody tension from the inside out, my fascia unwinding to release the energy of past traumas held in my physical body.

It is often said that in tai chi we try to move like water moves: flowing, gentle but powerful, able to yield around obstacles, without hesitation, without tension, effortless effort. The more I explore ancient styles of tai chi, the more I see how this powerful principle is used within the forms and the very movements in the forms. Our bodies move from our center, building circular, wave-like patterns of energy that flow out of our spiraling arms and hands. We become the gentle but powerful wave that moves through us as the form unfolds, allowing us to unfold in spiraling release. Eventually, the forms move us, not vice versa as the practice first begins.

These physical energetic practices connect us with the spiraling power of the chiForce that can be witnessed in both the large and small. No one would deny that the compact spiral of our DNA unfolds into the most complex organisms on the planet. The galaxies themselves spin out in spiraling swirls that are mimicked in the power of the spiraling hurricane or tornado. It is the curve that makes the difference. Most (all) energy moves in circular, spiral patterns. Light, sound, and electricity all move in waves. Mimicking these natural patterns of movement within tai chi forms (and surfing) allows us to connect on a very visceral level with the natural flow of the cosmos. We move away from our straight-lined cubicles and squarely laid-out-neighborhood grids with rectangular boxes and move in flowing arcs and curves that are more natural for our minds and bodies. This very natural physical flow creates our release into centeredness along the way. Flowing from the water within us, our energetic wave ripples out into the Sea of Chi, and gentle, spiraling waves of healing vibrations cascade through all the ocean's waves and all the ocean's shores.

Yesterday I paddled out at a popular surf spot just a little to my south, on some of the world's smallest waves. It was glorious! A little crowded now in the summer months—maybe thirty surfers out—but still plenty of elbow room on a small, glassy day. I spent about ninety minutes in the water, mostly just paddling hard to try to catch one of those tiny, long-rolling wavelets and failing in doing so all that often. In fact, in those ninety or so minutes in the water, I caught just one nice ride. The whole session, in fact the entire day, was a success thanks to that one wave.

Even though it would be called a small ankle- to knee-high wave, I was able to paddle efficiently so I could catch it soon enough that I had time to do a couple of little turns and cross-step up the nine-foot longboard toward the nose a little. It wasn't a powerful wave by any means, where I might have felt the powerful galactic chi rising through me. This was a relaxed, flowing, effortless ride. You know what I mean: easy, smooth, took no muscle whatsoever. What Lao Tzu would call effortless effort. Riding that wave left me with a sense of ease and flow in the world, of graceful presence and no need to rush for perfection, as now is enough.

You know this feeling. Athletes refer to it as the zone. Taoists call it being in the flow. If you've ever hit a baseball far into the outfield and it felt perfect and without effort, you've been in the flow. If you've ever served a tennis ball and heard and felt the perfect *pop* off the racquet with no impact into your wrist, you've been in the zone. If you've ever done anything, be it cooking, running, painting, drumming, where the outcome was perfect, the effort was relaxed, you didn't have to "work for it," and time ceased to exist, I think you've connected with the flowing effortlessness that is the nature of the real world.

Taoists always seek to live in this harmony, observing what is so and adjusting position accordingly, attempting to connect with the essence of each moment while staying in balance. When I catch just one perfect wave, my energy is changed; it becomes more in harmony with the current flowing moment. I synch up with the present galactic chi. When I practice tai chi and find the stillness within the motion, I am at one with the unified field, in the zone, fully present. This is the goal of all chi arts and the unspoken goal of the surfer: to connect fully with the galactic, universal energy.

The surfer practices mindfulness without often recognizing it as such. Absorbed into the moment—the flow of the current, the wave intervals, fish movement, balancing on the board, the position of other people in the water, the height of the swell, where the peak breaking point of the wave is—so much is taking the surfer's attention that all thoughts fade away and observation, fully *being*, takes their place. The surfer's mind must be fully present and not distracted to catch the wave and ride it. This is a moving meditation done in harmony with the flowing energy of the cosmos.

In the same way, tai chi practitioners engage in moving meditation when running forms. The tai chier is focusing internally instead of externally. Because of this internal focus, the goal is to know one's self fully, to be completely present in the physical body with every movement. All other thoughts are dispensed. This focus on inner awareness instead of outer awareness (which is most of our daily lives) puts responsibility on the self for how we move, breathe, and respond. Slowly, with practice and patience, we begin to understand how to move ourselves into the zone any time we choose, knowing we can control our internal space as we move through the external space of work, home, and all daily life. We learn self-responsibility and balance.

In a 1978 interview entitled "The Evolutionary Surfer," psychologist and writer Dr. Timothy Leary described surfing as "a merging of your own body neuromusculature, or brain body, with the power/energy/rhythm of nature. That's what's so jewel-like precise about mind/body/sea energy interfacing together. One thing I like about surfing is that it is all out. You can't be half-hearted, or you can't be thinking about something else. For one thing, the surfer is dealing with the most basic elements of all. There's almost no technology, and there's no symbolism. It's just the individual dealing with the power of the ocean, which gets into the power of lunar pulls, and of tidal ebbs and flows; and it's no accident that many, most, surfers have become mystics, or (I hate to use the word), spiritual. I prefer the word *neurological excursion*. But they've somehow been able to contact the infinity, and into the turbulence of the power of their own brain, and then they begin . . . see you can talk about surfing brain waves as you would about surfing external waves. There's purity about surfing. There's a profound sense of timing. Of course, if you study how evolution works and how the DNA code builds bodies and builds species, timing is of absolute importance. Being in the right place at the right time—it happens that whatever you do, you can't create a wave, you know; it comes and there's a time to move and a time to lay back. It's almost Taoist poetry. Almost Einsteinian."

Personally, I'd say it's exactly Taoist and exactly Einsteinian. The truth in nature is the truth in nature, however you want to spin it.

Knowing others is wisdom;
Knowing self is enlightenment.
Mastering others requires force;
Mastering self requires strength.
He who knows he has enough is rich.
—Lao Tzu, Tao Te Ching

As all things come and go, I left Satellite Beach when I could see the slow incoming wave of wealth begin to change the vibe and the rents. This came to the surface in a two-year time span during which several huge beachfront condominiums sprang up, blocking un-spoiled ocean views and limiting beach access; fancier city signs were installed, and many beach parks got facelifts with bathrooms, showers, new picnic-table areas, and of course updated signs. When I saw the installation of fancy street signs, I knew the end of my time here was close. Rents doubled in that two-year span and housing prices tripled, turning the entire area from a quaint, little seaside town with its own ocean-centric, comfortable style to looking and feeling a lot more generic but more like home to the many northerners moving in from the colder and more urban heartland. Such has been the fate of many former adorable and affordable towns in coastal places like Florida.

I moved off the barrier island, back to the small, space-centric town of Titusville where I had grown up, and I started a new job. I was trying to use what I'd learned and work smarter not harder. I think of energy efficiency as the same thing: smarter not harder. Surely all would agree that it's more intelligent and energy efficient to sail a boat than to row. In the same way, it's more intelligent and efficient to use the natural energy of sun, wind, and water than to use fossil fuels. Likewise, it is more intelligent for us as humans to get chores done using less energy. I kept reminding myself of this very fact when I moved my modest amount of stuff back to Titusville.

Typically, when I had moved in the past, I was sore for a day or more after from all the lifting, bending, and sheer physicality of moving stuff around. It always takes me a few days to recover from the fatigue and soreness. But this move I continually reminded myself, at times speaking the words aloud, "With as little effort as possible." All moving day long I reminded myself to use the tools I had cultivated: center, breathe, and lift using as little muscular effort as I could get away with to get the job done. I felt like I was practicing Tai Chi for Movers! I shouldn't have been, but I was amazed at the results. There was no soreness or fatigue from the move at all. In fact, I wasn't even tired after moving all the boxes, and I went for a walk after! The choice of effortless effort pays off.

One day a new coworker inadvertently pointed out something important to me: my life is epic because I surf. While training me, Susan mentioned she was about to go on a month-long kayaking trip around the tip of Florida. She said she wanted to "do something epic before I turn fifty!" It made me think: Here I am, nearing fifty myself, and I wonder if I will ever "settle down," because my entire life has been about life as an adventure. How far can I push myself? What new will I discover in a place I've never lived? Can I be a better person right now? For me, a big part of that adventure of the self was learning to surf and overcoming my self-limiting fear. When I mentioned to Susan that I surfed and we should go paddle together some time, she stopped in her tracks. "That's epic!" she exclaimed, surprised. I realized she was right. The very act of surfing on a regular basis has made my life an epic adventure, but the adventure reaches beyond surfing waves of water to surfing the Tao with each precious breath.

My daily adventure now has been to explore this place I once knew so well. I grew up here, close to the Kennedy Space Center, Merritt Island National Wildlife Refuge, the Intracoastal Waterway, and the isolated fifty-thousand-acre Canaveral National Seashore. As a young adult in this small town that boasts an immense variety of water activities, I lived in a family that didn't engage in any of them. Sure, we went fishing now and then on the Indian River Lagoon and had once-a-year bonfires on the public Satellite Beaches to the south, popping Jiffy Pop popcorn over the fire, but none of my family ever got in the water for fun, and the beach was so inaccessible that we rarely went there.

When I got my first car, the light-blue, squarish four-door family Dodge Diplomat, I made frequent jaunts to the closest beach: Canaveral National Seashore, also known as Playalinda. Because of its national park status, Playalinda Beach is a fee area (a big deterrent for my middle-income, indebted-to-the-American-dream parents). Because it sits just one mile or so from the Kennedy Space Center, when I was growing up Playalinda Beach was closed whenever rockets or shuttles launched or were preparing to launch. This meant that frequently no one could access the beach for over a month at a time.

As a child and on into high school, I heard rumors of big sharks, dangerous drop-offs, and unsafe conditions in the waters of Playalinda. Typically, there are no lifeguards on this protected, remote little tip of the barrier island that has been left as natural as Mother Nature intended. All natural except of course for the world headquarters of space exploration nearby, with the enormous Vehicle Assembly Building and the huge American flag on its side visible from miles and miles away. In my youth, when I drove past this building, to the beach, I was exploring my freedom within the world. I spent my beach time here walking the shoreline, not sunbathing nor getting in the water in any way. I walked for miles, alone and with friends, along the quiet, natural dune-lined shore.

The twenty-four-mile stretch of national seashore that incorporates Playalinda Beach is very isolated—no stores, no condominiums, no buildings of any kind. In fact, from town you must drive through the 140,000-acre Merritt Island National Wildlife Refuge, then across the 50,000-acre Cape Canaveral National Park just to get to the beach. There's only one heavily controlled single-lane road in and out of the beach area with designated parking lots. The road dead-ends after seven unshaded, blistering-hot miles of asphalt, but the beach itself can be walked much farther. No resources of any kind are available here, not even cell service usually. To my young mind, Playalinda was always kind of a dangerous place. I remember thinking how brave those beautiful surfer boys at school were to go out in that deep, foreboding, shark-infested water.

Whenever I think about those gorgeous surfer boys from high school, I think of how they moved. Part of their appeal, besides the obvious—their tan, athletic bodies—was that they exuded confidence in the way they stood and moved about. It was exactly like chi arts: feet planted, centered hips, heads up, shoulders back with chest and heart open to the world. And usually they were smiling. I noticed them long before I was able to articulate what it was about these young boys that so attracted me. I felt they had something special that others lacked: self-confidence and open hearts. Now I realize this is true of most dedicated surfers. This is part of the surf allure that can't be faked, bought, or sold. I remember thinking that surfing must really be something, for those beautiful, brave boys to be willing to risk all to ride a few waves.

Now here I am at forty-nine years old, surfing at Playalinda Beach as my home break. I am the first in my family to ever surf. They don't understand why I'm consumed by it. Living with a "new" beach, I must learn its conditions. Even though I'm only fifty miles north of where I learned to surf, the conditions are vastly different. It's not at all what I was led to believe it was, out here on the barren point of the island, the eastern-most point of the Florida peninsula that is Cape Canaveral. Fifty miles south, the beach faces due east. Here at Playalinda, due to the point of the cape, the beach faces a bit more northeasterly, so the currents and swells interact differently with the beach to create an entirely different wave condition than just slightly to the south at Cocoa or Satellite Beach.

Shifu Cook sent me a text not long ago, and the timing couldn't have been better. It said, "FEAR: Forget Everything and Run or Face Everything and Rise." He sent it during the first two weeks of my Playalinda Beach explorations.

In my youth I stayed far from the water because of my fear. Now, as a self-responsible adult, I looked my fear of Playalinda in the eye, facing it, not running. Because I had built up an expectation in my mind from the past of Playalinda being dangerous and sharky, I approached it with more caution than I would have any other beach that was new to me as a surfer. I approached with caution, but now I did not let my fear stop me.

My first session at Playalinda, I took a boogie board out instead of a surfboard, just to learn more about the conditions. Having more of my body in the water on the sponge board makes me feel more connected to how the energy is traveling through the water, so I understand how the wave is breaking better. It also affords me more opportunity to put my feet down and check out the bottom structure than when my whole body is floating on a surfboard.

I quickly realized that the fear I had of this place was only because I didn't understand it, and the hearsay evidence I had about it was false.

I had known this beach only as an outsider, one who walked along its shores but never fully immersed into the experience and energy of Playalinda that can only be found in its waters. It only took one session out on the boogie board to realize the bottom wasn't deep at all, as I had been told. Several people had told me that just ten to fifteen feet out from the sandy beach, the bottom dropped off to a big shelf where large sharks liked to hang out scouting for prey.

On one unusually bold day as a teenager I had tested this. It was a spectacular summer day; the ocean was calm and looked inviting. I was overheated from walking for hours. There were lots of other people wading in the water, so I thought I could handle it even though I lacked the comfort of companionship. Sure enough, just a few feet off shore I could no longer touch the bottom. I assumed what I had been told was true: a quick, deep drop-off was right there. Right away my fear took hold; my breathing became instantly shallow and panicky, while my heart thudded loudly in my ears. I got out of the water immediately that day.

Now, many years later, as a surfer I was exploring the bottom structure more thoroughly and boldly with only trace amounts of fear. I felt there was a bit of drop-off, but it was more like a small channel before the next sandbar. Then another seeming drop-off, which was just a trough in the sand that had naturally formed before the next sandbar farther out was built up again. I learned that what I had been told in my youth was not true at all. False evidence appearing real, or FEAR, had kept me from doing something I'd wanted to do my whole life. Now I realized that, unlike the rocky waters of Satellite Beach, the bottom at Playalinda is a series of sandbars and troughs, naturally creating good surf conditions.

Fifty miles south, around Cocoa Beach and Satellite Beach, the bottom is no longer very natural, as years of beach "restoration" projects have completely changed how the sand moves, or doesn't move, along the bottom. There are also some scattered reef systems to the south that keep getting devastated by the dredging and dumping of sand along the beaches to keep property safe from naturally eroding dunes. Why does the entire population pay for a few people to maintain dunes at their ocean-front homes? This is not in balance. Nor does the Army Corps of Engineers' Mid-Reach Restoration Project make sense for the ecology of the local shores. Those who live here, surf here, fish here, and boat here know it is a pure waste of money to dump millions of dollars of sand on the dunes only to have it wash right back out to sea. Sometimes that freshly laid sand, put down by a twenty-four-hour caravan of diesel-engine dump trucks, all washes out within one day because of the surf pulling it out to sea. This ongoing, million-dollar project doesn't make sense in any way, and as I had just learned, it doesn't help the surf conditions either.

No, the harsh conditions I had been warned about at wild, unrestored, all-natural Playalinda Beach didn't exist. Once I got in the water and explored, I realized all those warnings were false. It didn't take me long to see that the surf here is a little better than just a few miles to the south. The waves at Playalinda break more consistently due to the well-developed sandbar system, and there's no rocky reef that can swallow your unsuspecting leg and crack a dent into your surfboard. Another wonderful discovery from this new, old beach of mine is the water quality.

About twenty miles south of Canaveral National Seashore is the major East Coast shipping port of Port Canaveral. The entire beach area around Port Canaveral is quite urban: the famous roadway A1A lies just yards from the ocean sand there. The city streets have gutters leading directly to the ocean, as is the case continuing south down A1A to Cocoa Beach, Satellite Beach, and beyond. An enormous amount of street runoff from heavy rains goes directly into the ocean water where people and dolphins surf and play. So, the mindful surfer there notices the dirty water conditions after a rain. The water may smell funky, feel oily, and have street debris floating around. I've been out surfing there the day after an especially heavy all-day rain, and the water smelled and felt like oil, dirty motor oil. It was as though the heavy, pounding, all-day deluge on the hot asphalt washed all the oil out of heavily traveled A1A right into the ocean. I couldn't wait to get to the shower and soap!

This is not the case at the highly protected Canaveral National Seashore. Because it is on a barrier island that's a protected national park, there are no city streets that run off into the water. Here at Playalinda after a rain, the water is cleaner and clearer, more like the clear water associated with the Bahamas. What a joy to discover this!

Immersed in this translucent blue vibration, I become part of the crystalline, heavenly scene. The calming blue settles my mind, relaxes my breath, and leaves me wondering if I'm floating in the ocean or the sky. I have fully faced my fear, and I have learned that the fear was just my own ignorance. Once I had the courage to face what scared me the most, I began to learn about it, understand it, and then no longer fear it but respect it and be blessed by it with my epic daily life.

As I explored all the pull-outs along Playalinda's seven-mile stretch of road, I learned where the best surf spots were. The first day I went to the beach, I stopped at the very first parking pull-out, Lot #1, to observe the ocean from the high, exposed dune-top boardwalk. I was surprised at how nice the waves looked. But there was no one out in the water or on the beach yet, so I was hesitant to explore these unfamiliar waters with the boogie board I'd brought. As I sat high on that perch, I could see far out into the ocean. I could see dark areas in the clear water where schools of fish gathered. Scanning the scene, I spotted a small group of dolphins cruising north at a casual pace, interweaving between each other as they surfaced for life-giving air before plunging just beneath the surface again. Even though they appeared to be moving with purpose, as if they had somewhere to go, they sure looked like they were having fun getting there together.

Whether you can spot them or not, bottlenose dolphins are always present in the local ocean and river waters. When its windy and the water's surface is choppy or when it's overcast, spotting the small groups, and sometimes solo dolphins, as they surface to take a breath can be difficult. But these water ambassadors are always present. Here, on this high boardwalk perch overlooking the sea, I recalled how in the beginning I was so afraid of dolphins. I had visions of them sinking their big, round, piercing teeth into my paddling arm and powerfully pulling me under and out to sea. I had heard stories of this very thing happening to people in the nearby Bahamas. In the story it was always a big, solo male dolphin that overpowered the swimmer and pulled him out into the depths.

Now, having spent more time with these intelligent creatures in their own natural environment, I understand they are very curious and want to know what's in their living room. So they will swim right up to you to check you out. I've been startled when sitting out in the line-up numerous times by the forceful out-breath of a nearby-surfacing dolphin that came to see what I was. Even though they startled me, they never intimidated me the way the packs of human boys did. The dolphins were just curiously coming up to get an eye on me. Slowly I had begun to welcome the playful dolphin energy whenever I was out surfing. They reminded me to not take myself so seriously, to just relax, have fun, and enjoy the ride.

It wasn't long before a shaggy-haired fellow who had a surfboard in the bed of his truck made his way up the boardwalk to check the surf. Being the first surfer I had encountered at Playalinda, I asked him if he was from here. When he said yes, I asked the usual surfer local-knowledge questions: Where was the best longboard spot? How were the jellies? Were there showers or shade anywhere? Were there any sharks or other wildlife to worry about?

He was grateful to share what he had learned in over twenty-five years of surfing Playalinda Beach. It feels good to pass on acquired knowledge to those who are interested. When it came to my question about the sharks, he told me that in all the years he'd surfed here, he'd never heard of anyone having a shark encounter, let alone getting bit by one. All of my adolescent fears were unfounded. False Evidence Appearing Real. I was grateful he was willing to share his specialized local knowledge with me, an outsider from his perspective.

He sauntered back down the boardwalk in his flip-flops to the parking lot so he could drive a little further up the beach in search of a friend. With this new, welcomed information I decided to get the boogie board and plunge in alone. I was quite reserved at first. I waded in very, very slowly, only going out about waist deep and just catching a few small rides to release some of that fearful energy about this place from the past. Then I let myself fully play, enjoying a couple of hours of mid-tide boogie boarding, smiling and laughing all the way.

By the time I got out of the water that first day at Playalinda, more people were on the beach. As I walked to the boardwalk, smiling broadly with my sponge board under one arm and flippers in the other hand, sand grinding against my skin on the inside of my tight rash guard, an older guy commented that I sure was having fun out there. He looked as though he might have caught some of my stoke just from watching me play in the water. I felt like I had released my stifled inner child who had been held back from enjoying Playalinda all these years. While there were other people fishing, sunbathing, and walking on the beach there at Lot #1, I was the only person in the water while I was there that day. Me and the dolphins, breathing, letting go, and enjoying the energy of the moment. *Doo be do be do.*

After my short learning curve at the isolated Playalinda Beach, I went out to surf there as much as I could. There had been a long flat spell with no waves for three weeks. I still went out to the beach at sunrise to play tai chi and swim, watching the weather and surf reports intently, praying for surf, as all the local wave-riders were. I saw in the weather report that a small low-pressure system was rolling in from the south overnight. I decided to get up early to see if I could catch a few sunrise waves before work.

I woke at 5:30 a.m., stashed my nine-foot longboard into the hatchback of my economy car (it just barely fit), and drove into the dark morning, hoping to greet the sunrise on the beach with favorable surf conditions. I was the first person on the beach that day. I waited as the national park ranger on duty opened the gates to collect fees and let people into the park. "Have fun," he said, smiling, as I pulled through, flashing my yearly pass. It was still dark out, with just a soft line of light breaking along the brightening horizon.

I sat on the boardwalk for a minute or two, surveying the conditions in the water below. It was about two hours before low tide. In the darkness, I could just make out silhouettes of small waves rolling in gently. I went back to the car to get my surfboard and leash. Facing my lifelong fears, I paddled into the dark unlit water alone at sunrise with no other person for miles and miles. I slowly glided out into the ocean, letting myself get pulled along the glassy surface, feeling the currents beneath my belly and board. In a favorable spot I stopped paddling and sat up, letting my bare legs dangle, relaxed, into the dark depths below.

The sunrise was overwhelming in its slow, patient display of cloud-smeared oranges, pinks, and reds. The glassy water reflected the intense colors as they became more defined. I was floating in a vast ocean of slightly swaying, warm, liquid color. It was remarkable and soothing. Surveying the scene, I turned, looking back to shore, and saw I was indeed all alone. No one was within sight in either direction down the shoreline, and no cars had been in any of the parking areas as I drove down to Lot #6. I was so immersed in the grandeur of the moment that at the time I didn't even realize that I was experiencing no hint or thought of fear. In that moment, it all came full circle. I was at ease, at one, in the flow, solely responsible for myself. I felt blessed by all of creation, saturated in the Glory of the Unified Field of Being.

I paddled gently into my first small wave that day, silently popped up onto my feet, and caught a perfect, tiny, knee-high long-roller. As the wave's energy slowly unwound, I was able to cross-step gingerly toward the front of the board, mindfully placing each foot into position before lifting the other. Before I even knew it, I had tai chi walked up the center stringer of the board and touched the toes of my right foot on the nose of the board for a fraction of a second before I had to retreat to maintain balance on the small wave that was ending. I could have ridden it all the way onto the sand, as I had connected immediately with the curl, the center of the cosmic chi that drove the wave forward. Instead, I turned out of the ride perfectly, shifting all of my weight to my back foot to sink the tail section of the board so it would turn on a pivot 180 degrees back out to sea. I gently laid my belly down on the floating platform and casually paddled back out past the break zone, allowing the backflow of the wave's energy to carry me a little. It took just four or five paddle strokes to return to where I had begun the ride.

Salt water stung my eyes as it rolled down my face into my open, smiling mouth. My long, stringy, untethered, wet hair now covered my eyes like flowing curtains. In my blindness, I could finally see where I was. I had put my toes on the nose. On the first wave of the day I had hung five for the first time in my almost-fifty-year-old life. It was only a fraction of a moment. No one saw it but me and the ocean.

As I sat there, arms stretched wide in gratitude, smiling from ear to ear, watching the sun rise from the kaleidoscopic, morphing water I floated in, a family of dolphins surfaced nearby. They glided so efficiently and effortlessly through the sea we now shared that there was not even a ripple to give away their hidden presence. It was the sound of their powerful breath that I noticed first, not a disturbance in the glassy rainbow water we shared. When one of them stuck its head out of the water remarkably close by to check me out, it felt like my accomplishment was being recognized by Mother Nature herself.

Here, alone, at the breaking of a new day, sharing waves and breaths with dolphins, I realized that I had come full circle and was exactly where I should be. In the infinite present of the moment, I realized that everything I ever needed or wanted was always there for me. With the bright clarity of the sun now shining directly into my eyes, I recognized that all my life it's been up to me which wave to ride.

Feeling another swell rising, I turn to shore, a soul surfer paddling for the privilege of riding another ripple of galactic chi. The outline of another longboarder moves down the boardwalk toward the beach. I'm grateful we get to ride some waves together, creating and sharing the vibrations of a new day.

Tai Chi and Qigong Resources

Lea Williamson's website, where you can sign up for free newsletters, view online training videos, and connect to Lea's blog: www.BeachsideQigong.com

Grand Master Jeffery B. Cook: traditional martial arts training in the Arlington, VA area. www.TTTPerformanceMartialArts.com

Dr. Paul Lam, founder of www.TaiChiforHealthInstitute.com. Here you can find Tai Chi for Health instructor training, online video lessons, and certified teachers worldwide.

www.WorldTaiChiDay.com has numerous free resources to promote tai chi and qigong; an excellent instructor resource with many practice videos.

Lao Tzu. *Tao Te Ching, A New Translation by Gia-Fu Feng and Jane English. Vintage Books, 1972.*

Surfrider Foundation: www.Surfrider.org, where you can learn to be more ocean minded.

BE THE SOLUTION

Lea Williamson's Author Bio

Lea Williamson is a longboard surfer, shifu (expert) of qigong, certified tai chi and qigong instructor, licensed clinical massage therapist, and Reiki master who has been practicing daily tai chi and qigong for over twenty-five years. A Florida Space Coast native, she teaches workshops and private and group sessions in the beautiful parks of Brevard County and elsewhere. It is her mission to share the ancient healing arts of tai chi and qigong so many more can experience their lasting benefits.

.

CPSIA information can be obtained
at www.ICGtesting.com
Printed in the USA
LVHW090337080120
642879LV00001B/191/P